# THE TOTALLY UNAUTHORIZED

# Microsoft® Joke Book™

## Second Edition

Created, Collected and Edited

by

Tim Barry

**TOTALLY**
## The Unauthorized Microsoft Joke Book - 2nd Edition

The Totally Unauthorized Microsoft Joke Book™
Second Edition

web site: www.msjokebook.com

10 9 8 7 6 5 4 3 2 1

ISBN: 0-966-74171-4

Second Edition cover design by Foster and Foster, Inc.

THE TOTALLY

# UNAUTHORIZED
## Microsoft Joke Book™

## Second Edition

### Table of Contents

TOTALLY
The↗ Unauthorized Microsoft Joke Book - 2<sup>nd</sup> Edition

## Preface to the Second Edition

How times have changed since we published our first edition of "The Totally Unauthorized Microsoft Joke Book" back in April, 1999. Y2K ended up a non-event. The Internet grew pervasive even as the Internet stock bubble burst. State and federal challenges to some of Microsoft's business practices have continued on relentlessly. The overall economy has slowed into recession. And, of course, September 11 made terrorism a household word.

As the times have changed, so too have the "shakers and movers" in business and government. Over 40% of the celebrities used in the jokes have changed jobs and/or titles. Bill Clinton, Al Gore and Janet Reno all have moved on and in their places we now have George W. Bush, Dick Cheney and John Ascroft. The good news: the new players are all pretty funny, too. The net effect of all of these changes is that while Microsoft remains a technology market force of immense power, the company now finds itself operating in a business landscape which has changed significantly.

In preparing the second edition of this collection we added lots of new material. We also updated the contemporary references to match changes in people or circumstances – which in some cases significantly changed the "look and feel" of a joke. The update of the "Microsoft Goes Nuclear" mock news story on page 18, when compared to the version in the first edition, is an example of how changing times significantly changed the joke.

Overall, the second edition has over 15% more pages and well over 70% of the material is new or updated so you'll need to have both editions to have all of the versions of all of the jokes. The goal, however, remains the same: poke a little good natured fun at Microsoft.

TOTALLY
The ↗ Unauthorized Microsoft Joke Book - 2ⁿᵈ Edition

## 1.0 Introduction to the Second Edition

The penalty of being one of the biggest, baddest and best known companies in high technology is often notoriety and, in the case of Microsoft, that notoriety pervades both the technical and the business worlds. And, as is often the case, this notoriety leads in turn to the (usually unwanted) attention of humorists and critics. Microsoft is just plain too big, too successful and, well, just too darn serious about itself not to make a really great target for jokes of all sizes and shapes.

This is a collection of humor about Microsoft. The company. The products. Windows. The company culture. Bill Gates, himself. Many of these have never been published before. And, while there still isn't a single "How many programmers does it take to change a light bulb" joke in the main Microsoft chapters, we have listened to reader feedback. So, by popular demand, in the second edition we've added an entire bonus chapter with 101 of the best light bulb jokes we've heard.

Even humorous items you may have heard before or seen floating around on the Internet have some new twists and, as you read, you'll notice appearances by celebrities - both from inside and outside the information technology industry - to further liven up the material.

We hope techies and non-techies (maybe even some at Microsoft) will enjoy this collection of material and view it not as mean spirited but rather in the true tradition of Jonathon Swift, Sinclair Lewis, *National Lampoon* and other purveyors of parody and satire, namely using humor to prod at the foibles and fumbles of the rich and famous.

✦ ✦ ✦

## 2.0  Microsoft Company Culture

**Q.** What's the difference between Microsoft employees and members of a religious cult?

**A.** Members of religious cults usually get at least one day per week off to rest.

Andy Grove, Chairman of Intel Corporation, was working in his office when his secretary buzzed to inform him that he had two very important visitors waiting.

"Who are they?" asked Grove.

"The Pope and Bill Gates," replied his secretary.

"Send in the Pope first," sighed Grove, "I only have to kiss his ring."

We understand that there is no truth to the rumor that a Microsoft programmer who tried to use "penis" as his system password had it rejected as, "Too short".

**Q.** What's the best thing to throw to a drowning Microsoft Windows programmer?

**A.** A Macintosh.

## Test if you might be Microsoft employee material:

1. Have you ever debated the merits of Jolt Cola versus Mountain Dew for all night programming gigs?

2. Do you actually know what "HTTP", "HTML", "TCP/IP", "ISDN" AND "ISP" mean?

3. Do you know more about MIPS than MPG?

4. Does your wrist watch have more computing power than a 1.6Ghz Athlon™ CPU?

5. Can you identify any original Star Trek episode from a random 10 second clip?

6. Do computer store salespeople ask you questions?

7. Do you get up at 3:00 AM to go to the bathroom and stop to check your email on the way back to bed?

8. Do you think that being "multi-lingual" means programming in C++, HTML, PERL and Visual Basic?

9. Do you have more friends on the Internet than in real life?

10. Do you know the difference between the Internet and real life?

11. Do you have six or more email addresses?

12. Do you think the 4 basic food groups are caffeine, sugar, chocolate and pork rinds?

If you answered yes to eight or more questions, you may have what it takes to work at Microsoft.

**Q.** What did they do to the Microsoft programmer who started to take Viagra?

**A.** Transferred him to the hardware group.

A rather inhibited Microsoft systems programmer finally cashed in some stock options and splurged on a luxury cruise. It was the "craziest" thing he had ever done in his life. Unfortunately, just as he was beginning to relax and enjoy himself, a typhoon struck the ship and it quickly capsized and sank. Unconscious, the programmer washed ashore alone on a secluded island.

Outside of the lush tropical beauty, a fresh water spring, and trees bearing mangos, bananas and coconuts, there was little else. He lost all hope and for hours on end sat forlornly watching the horizon for any sign of a ship. One day, long after losing track of time, he was stunned to see a beautiful woman rowing toward shore in a small rowboat.

"I'm from the other side of the island," she said. "Were you on the cruise ship, too?"

"Yes, I was," he answered. "Where did you find the rowboat?"

"Well, I carved the oars from tree branches, wove the siding from the tall native grass and made the keel and stern from a palm tree blown down by the storm."

"But, what did you use for tools?" asked the programmer.

"I think pirates visited this island long ago. I found an old cutlass and a knife alongside a skeleton with a missing leg. But, enough of that. Where have you been living all this time? I don't see any shelter."

"To be honest, I've just been sleeping in a lean to just up from the beach," he said.

"Let's go back to my place." the woman offered.  As she rowed them around to her side of the island the programmer was amazed to see a sturdy two story bungalow.

"It's pretty basic, but I call it home." Once inside, she said,

"Would you like a drink?"

"No, thanks," said the programmer.  "I can't stand the thought of any more coconut juice!"

"It's not coconut juice, you silly.  I ferment it out back, so we can have coconut wine." The programmer accepted the drink, which to his amazement tasted like a fine Chardonnay, and they sat down on her couch to talk.  After comparing stories of the shipwreck, she asked, "Would you like to take a shower?"

"Yes," the programmer replied eagerly, "I've had to get by with rinsing in the stream."

"Well, if you'd like, there's a shower upstairs in the bathroom."

The programmer, still amazed, went upstairs to the bathroom and showered, cleaning himself with a homemade bar of pumice soap and all the while wondering how the hot water was being piped to the shower. He even managed to shave with a razor made from a clam shell. Feeling clean and refreshed for the first time in months he headed back downstairs.

"That's much better," said the woman. "I think I'll go and slip into something more comfortable."

While she changed the programmer continued to sip his wine.  She returned a short time later wearing a sexy teddy fashioned out of woven grass.  "Tell me," she asked, "we've both been here alone for a long time.  Have you been lonely...is there anything that you really, *really* miss?  Something that all men and woman need?"

"Yes there is!" the programmer replied, becoming bolder. "There is something I've missed for so long. But on this island all alone, I had given it up as just impossible."

"Well, it's not impossible, now," the woman purred.

The programmer, practically panting in his excitement, said breathlessly: "You mean you've actually figured out how we can get on the Internet and check our e-mail from here?"

**Q.** What do you need when you have a Microsoft software license negotiating team up to their necks in concrete?

**A.** More concrete.

Microsoft group vice president Jeff Raikes was in New York to brief nervous information technology industry analysts regarding the status of the ongoing Microsoft anti-trust litigation. Later, he was asked "How did your meeting with the analysts go?" by Neil Cavuto on Fox News Network.

"Just fine," replied the satisfied Raikes, "We had a very good discussion and a frank exchange of views. The analysts came in with their views and they left with ours."

A little girl asked her father, "Daddy, do all fairy tales begin with, 'Once upon a time'?"

"No sweetie," replied Dad. "A lot of fairy tales begin with, 'Thank you for buying this quality Microsoft product. Your satisfaction is very important to us...'."

# 10 ways things would be different if Microsoft was from Texas:

10. Dialog boxes would give you the choice of "Yup", "Nope", or "Git"

9. The Windows recycle bin would be an outhouse instead of a waste basket

8. Flight Simulator would be replaced by Mud Pit Tractor Pull simulator

7. Windows splash screen would feature Texas flag

6. Microsoft mouse would be an armadillo

5. Windows XP theme song would be "How Do You Like Me Now?" instead of "Ray of Light"

4. Corporate campus would have hitching posts, salt licks and hay bales

3. Four words:  Dallas Cowboys Cheerleaders Screensaver

2. Wait icon would be an empty beer bottle instead of an hourglass

1. Chairman would be Billy-Joe-Jim-Bob (a.k.a. Bubba) Gates

With all the wealth created by stock options, some Microsoft employees became a bit materialistic. A marketing executive and a development vice president were comparing the features of their huge new sport utility vehicles.

"Nice SUV," said the marketer. "Fully loaded?"

"Yes, I think so."

"I've got a two channel cell phone with fax and wireless remote Internet hookup," pointed out the marketer, looking for a feature his friend might have missed.

"Me, too."

"Got a television?"

"Of course," replied the development VP, getting into the spirit of the game. "I've got a full home theater setup with sixteen speakers."

"Got a bed?" asked the marketing exec.

"Uh, No. You've got a bed??"

"Yeah, I had to have it put in custom but it's a really cool feature," replied the marketer, thrilled to have found something that he had and his friend didn't. "Now when I work late I can crash right here and I don't have to drive home."

Really put out at being 'out featured', the development VP went back to the SUV dealer and demanded that a custom bed be installed.

A couple weeks later, working late as usual, the developer noticed the marketing executive's vehicle in the parking lot. The lights were on and he could hear the stereo playing. Unable to resist, he stopped and knocked on the window. No response. He knocked louder. No response. Anxious to show that he has caught up in the feature race, he pounded on the door. Finally, the marketing guy rolled down the window and asked, "What do you want?"

"Hi," began the development VP. "I just wanted to tell you that now I've got a bed in my SUV, too, and mine has deep heat and a built in variable speed massager."

"Do you mean to tell me that you got me out of the hot tub just to tell me that?"

Competition for the top jobs at Microsoft can be really tough. To make it to the top you have to demonstrate talent, ability, aggressiveness and, perhaps most important, total, unswerving loyalty to Microsoft. For one particularly plum assignment the selection process had narrowed down to three candidates. All had been with Microsoft for some time and all had impeccable credentials. Each was to be given a final two hour stress interview and the final selection made. As part of the final interview process each had been requested to bring their spouse along.

With his wife waiting in the lobby, the first candidate went in for his stress interview. At the end of the interview, one of the interviewers began his summary. "You are a great candidate. As one final test of your total loyalty to Microsoft take this gun, go into the lobby, shoot your wife and the job will be yours."

Taken aback, the candidate jumped to his feet, shouted, "You must be out of your mind! I love my wife madly. We have two small children. I could never hurt her. TAKE THIS JOB AND SHOVE IT!!" and sprinted out the door never to be seen again.

The second candidate arrived and went in for her interview. At the end of the interview, the lead interviewer gave the same summary:

"You are a great candidate. As one final test of your total loyalty to Microsoft take this gun, go into the lobby, shoot your husband and the job will be yours."

Thinking about it for several minutes, the candidate finally replied, "I know the job requires a lot of loyalty and I can see how you would use a pressure situation like this to test it, but I really don't think I can do it. My husband and I have been together for many years, we're very comfortable together and the promotion is just not worth it to me. I'll just stay where I am. Please withdraw my name from further consideration." She then got up and left to return to her office.

The third candidate arrived and went in for his interview. As before, at the end of the interview the lead interviewer gave his summary: "You are a great candidate. As one final test of your total loyalty to Microsoft take this gun, go into the lobby, shoot your wife and the job is yours."

Without hesitation the candidate got up, took the gun and headed back to the lobby.

BANG. . . . . .BANG, BANG, BANG, BANG, BANG.

THUMP. . . . . .THUMP, THUMP, THUMP, THUMP.

Upon re-entering the interview room, the confused interviewer asked the disheveled and out of breath candidate, "What the hell was all that THUMPING?"

"Oh, that," responded the candidate while calmly combing his hair and straightening his clothes, "Some moron put blanks in the gun. Scared her good, but I had to finish her off with a lobby chair."

The world's most famous software oxymoron:  Microsoft Works

Microsoft President Steve Ballmer and Chief Operating Officer Robert Herbold were out hiking in the Pacific Northwest woods one afternoon when they found their path blocked by a huge bear. They reversed course immediately but were dismayed to find that the bear was following them and looking most unfriendly. Herbold quickly stopped, took off his day pack, removed his mountain hiking boots and started to put on his running shoes.

"Bob," said Ballmer - a much stronger runner, "This is random. Forget it. You can't possibly outrun a bear."

"Steve," said Herbold - a much more analytical thinker, "I don't have to outrun the bear. I just have to outrun you."

✦ ✦ ✦

## Microsoft Marketing Haikus

Crushed and broken
competitors beg for mercy.
Another good day.

Justice department
offered another deal today.
Like, as if we care.

Maintenance release
has more bugs than original code.
Nobody is surprised.

Windows XP is
hailed as a major advance.
We own the press corps.

✦ ✦ ✦

# 10 Suggestions for a kinder, gentler Microsoft public image:

10. Bundle CD of "Don't Worry, Be Happy" with each copy of Windows XP

9. Charity benefit softball game with justice department lawyers

8. X-Box version of *Who Wants to be a Millionaire?* with real prizes

7. Lots of photo ops for Steve Ballmer with Mr. Rogers

6. Special "We love Microsoft" episode of *Barney and Friends*

5. Donate some of the billions of dollars in their cash hoard to feed the homeless instead of developing the next piece of superfluous bloatware (OOPS, a serious one slipped in. Sorry!)

4. Hire the Dali Lhama as spokesperson

3. Try doing more and announcing less

2. Two words:  eschew obfuscation

1. Two more words:  play fair

✦ ✦ ✦

## MICROSOFT GOES NUCLEAR

REDMOND, WASHINGTON (AP) -- The world was stunned today as Microsoft became the world's first publicly traded nuclear power by detonating an underground nuclear test at a secret facility in eastern Washington state. The detonation, which occurred just after dawn at 5:40 am Pacific Time, appears to have been timed to coincide with talks between Microsoft and the United States Department of Justice over ongoing anti-trust litigation.

"Microsoft will defend our right to market our products and destroy our competitors by any and all means necessary," said Microsoft Chairman and CEO Bill Gates. "We have an obligation to our shareholders to continue to increase shareholder value. We will do everything in our power to advance our business objectives and we want the government to realize that there are significant risks associated with interfering in our business."

The test was conducted at a remote site on the Hanford Nuclear Reservation, which Microsoft recently acquired from the U.S. Government. Scientists at Los Alamos estimated the yield of the explosion at approximately 50 kilotons and sources at the Department of Energy have confirmed that, due to the acquisition of Hanford and the surrounding 'highly enriched' acreage, Microsoft probably has access to enough weapons grade plutonium for several more devices.

In a related story, rumors have surfaced of a second secret weapons development project underway at Microsoft. While details remain sketchy, highly placed sources indicate that the program may be based on technology originally developed by Microsoft for its ill fated BOB program manager. "BOB was the biggest bomb to hit the software industry in the 90's," said one knowledgeable industry source who spoke on a condition of anonymity. "The damage was incredible. I'd sure hate to be around if they drop that baby again."

In Washington, after an emergency meeting of the National Security Council, President Bush immediately announced that in response to the Microsoft test the U.S. Government would boycott all Microsoft products. Later, the President appeared at a press conference and dismissed the Microsoft test as an empty threat.

"Who does this little dweeb Gates think he is?" said the President. "He may have the bomb but I've got armored divisions, F-16s, stealth bombers and the U.S. Marines. That Microsoft campus looks like a rest area compared to Afghanistan. If the Taliban and al-Qaida leadership couldn't hide for long in caves in Tora Bora I doubt that Mr. Gates and his senior staff can hide out very long in Redmond. Don't mess with Texas."

Sources in the administration said they plan to have "frank discussions" with Microsoft to defuse this dangerous situation. This will hopefully lead to Microsoft's agreement to cease testing and sign the Nuclear Non-Proliferation Treaty. Eventually it is hoped that Microsoft and the government will engage in productive disarmament talks.

Bill Gates was unavailable for comment on President Bush's remarks.

Microsoft stock (MSFT - NASDAQ) closed down 2-1/2 points on active trading.

Of course, then there was the Microsoft programmer who started taking Viagra and went from Microsoft to macrohard.

# 10 Things Microsoft will never admit in public:

10. Tried to get Washington state bird changed to Microsoft mouse

9. Secretly owns 25% of worldwide hard disk manufacturing capacity

8. Tried to buy the Internet back in 1986

7. Offered to finance Mars landing for NASA if they would rename the red planet to 'Gates World'

6. Offered Pope $1 billion for exclusive online rights to the Apocalypse for MSNBC

5. Has secret research project to see if programmers can be cloned

4. Has really secret legal research project to see if clones share original programmers stock options or must be given their own

3. Buying Area 51 for new advanced development site

2. Rejected Chinese offer to trade Hong Kong for a nationwide Windows XP site license

1. Three words:  guilty as charged

✦ ✦ ✦

Knowing that new employees are the key to the company's future, every spring Microsoft spends a great deal of time and money sending representatives to college campuses to recruit the best young engineering talent. Reaching the end of a job interview, one recruiter asked a particularly promising young software engineer due to graduate from MIT, "What sort of starting salary were you thinking about?"

After thinking a few moments the fledgling software developer replied, "In the neighborhood of $125,000 a year, depending on the benefits package."

The recruiter said, "Well, what would you say to a package with $125,000 base salary, quarterly bonuses, five weeks vacation, twelve paid holidays, full medical, dental, vision, life and disability insurance, a Microsoft 401(K) retirement fund where we match up to 50% of your contribution, generous stock options and a new leased company car every two years - say, a Porsche Boxster S?"

The young software engineer, thinking she had hit the mother lode, sat up straight and said, "Wow! Are you kidding?"

"Yeah", the recruiter replied, "But you started it."

Q.    What's the difference between a used car salesman and a computer store salesperson explaining a new Microsoft product?

A.    The used car salesman knows he's lying - and he can probably drive a car.

**Q.** You're trapped in an elevator with a crazed serial killer, Osama bin Laden and a Microsoft level 15 software architect. Unfortunately, your gun only has two bullets. What do you do?

### Pre-September 11, 2001 answer:

**A.** Save the computer industry - shoot the software architect twice!!

### Post September 11, 2001 answer:

**A.** Save the world - shoot Osama bin Laden twice then beat him some more with the gun butt.

The following email was received at the Microsoft Human Resource center:

Date:  Mon, 08 Oct 2001 13:10:03 -0800
To:    personnelreviews@microsoft.hr.com
From:  amanager@microsoft.dev.com
RE:    Performance review for Nathan H...

While working as Nathan's supervisor, I usually find him working studiously and efficiently at his workstation without gossiping with other workers in the department. He never spends time on useless tasks. When assigned work, he always finishes his assignments on time. A loner, Nathan is most often working in his office engrossed in projects and he is never found wasting time playing online games. He has absolutely no problems with his peers despite his high levels of skill and deep knowledge of this technical field. I strongly feel he should be promoted and in the event of any downsizing he should not be terminated or reassigned.

Not long thereafter, a second email arrived:

Date:  Mon, 08 Oct 2001 13:52:03 -0800
To:    personnelreviews@microsoft.hr.com
From: amanager@microsoft.dev.com
RE:   Earlier email performance review for Nathan H....

Nathan was standing in my office looking at my computer screen when I was typing the email performance review sent to you earlier today. For my <u>true</u> assessment of this cretin read only every other line - i.e. 1,3,5,7...

The Pacific Northwest is not always a pleasant place to be in the dead of winter. One bitter afternoon as the winds howled, the rain pelted and the temperature dropped, an electrician at a construction project on the Microsoft campus noticed an ironworker stop what he was doing, climb down off the building and walk away.

"Where are you going?" the electrician called out.

"To get my heavy jacket."

"Where is it?"

"In San Diego," yelled the ironworker as he climbed into his pickup and sped off.

Popular bumper sticker in Redmond, Washington:

**WE ARE MICROSOFT. RESISTANCE IS FUTILE.**
**YOU WILL BE ASSIMILATED.**

# 10 New Year's Resolutions for Microsoft:

**For Next Year We will...**

10. Develop a Windows naming convention that makes sense...and stick with it

9. Work harder at maintaining the illusion that we compete fairly

8. Listen to the entire complaint before we explain why it's not our fault

7. Stop touting product features before the product development has actually started

6. Cut press releases by 25%, thereby saving countless acres of trees

5. Keep repeating: "We don't own the Internet. We don't own the Internet. We don't own..."

4. Hold the technical support call primary wait queue under 2 hours

3. Not publicly thumb our nose at the Department of Justice

2. Take ourselves less seriously

1. Keep the other nine resolutions past January 2

A male programmer was walking across Microsoft's Redmond campus one day when, to his surprise, he heard a frog call out to him from a shrub and say, "If you kiss me, I'll turn into a beautiful princess."

Intrigued, he bent over, picked up the frog, put it in his pocket and continued on his walk. After a while, the frog spoke up again and said, "If you kiss me, I'll turn back into a princess. I'm 19, I'm beautiful and I'll be your girl friend for the next month." The programmer took the frog out of his pocket, smiled, stroked it lovingly and gently returned it to his pocket.

Still later, the frog spoke up again, "Look, if you kiss me, I'll turn back into a princess. I'm 19, I'm beautiful, I'm incredibly sexy and I'll be your love slave for a year and do anything, and I mean ANYTHING, you want." Again the programmer took the frog out, smiled, stroked it lovingly and gently returned it to his pocket.

Finally, the frustrated frog screamed, "WHAT IS YOUR PROBLEM? I've told you I'm a beautiful, sexy princess. I've told you that I'll stay with you for a year. I've told you that I'll do anything you want. Why won't you kiss me?"

Finally, the programmer took the frog out, gazed into its eyes and said, "Look, I'm a software developer at Microsoft. There is no way I have time for a girlfriend, let alone a love slave, but having a talking frog is, like, really cool."

**Q.** Bill Gates, Steve Ballmer and senior members of the Windows development team are in a sinking boat. Who gets saved?

**A.** The software industry.

**10 spokespeople Microsoft rejected as, "Sending the wrong message":**

10. Conan the Barbarian

9. Lady Macbeth

8. Torquemada

7. Q

6. Jack Kevorkian

5. Jabba the Hut

4. The Alien

3. Damien Thorne

2. Darth Vader

1. The Terminator

✦ ✦ ✦

## 10 favorite internal Microsoft company songs:

10. "The Codes Are All Right" (sung to "The Kids Are All Right")

9. "If I Had a Spammer" (sung to "The Hammer Song")

8. "Onward Windows Programmers" (sung to "Onward Christian Soldiers")

7. "When the Geeks Go Marching In" (sung to "When the Saints Go Marching In")

6. "Microsoft oh Microsoft" (sung to "Christmas Tree o' Christmas Tree")

5. "Look at Me, The Browser's Free" (sung to "Look at Me, I'm Sandra Dee")

4. "I Heard It Through The Web Line" (sung to "I Heard It Through The Grapevine")

3. "Six T-1's" (sung to "Sixteen Tons")

2. "Microsoft is Coming to Town" (sung to "Santa Claus is coming to Town")

1. "Windows, Windows Uber Alles" (sung to "Deutchland, Deutchland, Uber Alles")

## Microsoft Staff Performance Review Secret Meanings

| Review Term | Secret Meaning |
| --- | --- |
| Good presentation skills | Runs PowerPoint |
| Excellent presentation skills | Bullshits and runs Power Point |
| Good communication skills | Spends lots of time on phone |
| Well qualified | Related to a senior manager |
| Exceptionally well qualified | Married to a senior manager |
| Work is first priority | Has no life |
| Socially active | Drinks a lot |
| Family is socially active | Spouse drinks a lot, too |
| Works well independently | Nobody knows what they do |
| Highly intelligent | Wears glasses |
| Quick thinking | Always has a good excuse |
| Confrontational style | Punches co-workers |
| Very confrontational style | Punches boss |
| Thoughtful | Sleeps at desk |
| Analytical | Can't make a decision |
| Careful | Won't make a decision |
| Aggressive | Obnoxious |
| Technically proficient | Reads instruction manuals |
| Delegates well | Gets someone else to do work |
| Good verbal expression skills | Speaks English |
| Good written expression skills | Can use spell checker |
| Attentive to details | Nit picker |
| Highly attentive to details | Anal retentive nit picker |
| Good leadership qualities | Intimidates others |
| Good judgement | Flips coin to makes decision |
| Exceptionally good judgment | Agrees with boss's decisions |
| Team player | Ass kisser |
| Strong team player | Exceptionally good ass kisser |
| Good sense of humor | Laughs at bosses jokes |
| Career minded | Back stabber |
| Loyal | Stock options not vested yet |

✦ ✦ ✦

## 3.0    Big, Bad Bill, Part I

How about that major blunder at the U.S. Postal Service?  They printed a stamp honoring Microsoft and Bill Gates only to discover that people from the personal computer industry were spitting on the wrong side!!

A research psychologist, curious to see if the pets of famous people picked up any of the traits of their celebrity owners, borrowed the cats of basketball superstar Michael Jordan, supermodel Cindy Crawford and Bill Gates.  Releasing Michael Jordan's cat into a room with a variety of cat toys, a large mouse, a bowl of food and a cat box, the researcher watched with interest through a one way mirror as the cat ignored the food and the mouse while proceeding to expertly dribble a small ball around the room.

He next released Cindy Crawford's cat into the room.  It completely ignored the other cat, turned up its nose at the mouse and the food, sauntered over to the mirror and began to contentedly preen itself.

He next released Bill Gates's cat into the room.

Without hesitation the cat screwed both the other cats, killed the mouse, ate all the food then pulled out the copy of *InfoWorld* lining the litter box and began to read intently.

You be the judge.

Stepping out of the shower one morning, Bill Gates slipped on the wet tile and fell to the tile floor with a loud 'thud'.

"MY GOD, are you all right," screamed his wife.

"Melinda, dear," said Bill as he staggered to his feet rubbing his head, "When we're alone you know you can just call me 'Bill'."

# 10 Titles rejected for Bill Gates autobiography:

10. *My Way on the Information Superhighway*

9. *Miles To Go Before I Sleep*

8. *The Future is Mine - I Bought It*

7. *Blood and Bits*

6. *Bill Gates and the Stoned Sorcerers*

5. *The Baudfather*

4. *Revenge of the Nerds, Final Chapter*

3. *The Money is the Reward*

2. *The Nerdict*

1. *B is for Billionaire*

✦ ✦ ✦

A Microsoft security guard caught two non-employees playing volleyball on the campus volleyball court in the middle of the afternoon and immediately ordered them off the campus.

"How did you know they weren't our employees?" asked Bill Gates while commending the guard for his heads up performance.

"Two ways, sir: they knew how to play and they had tans."

Rush Limbaugh, Bill Maher and Bill Gates were en route to Washington D.C. when the airplane in which they were riding crashed. Limbaugh and Maher find themselves in the judgment hall of Purgatory, but Gates is nowhere to be seen. After an interminable wait, each in turn approaches the dais to hear his sentence.

"Rush Limbaugh," a basso profundo voice boomed, "In penance for your sins you are required to spend the next 10 years as the off air studio engineer for Howard Stern's daily radio show – but you will not be allowed to do any 'on air' talking."

"Bill Maher," the voice continued, "In penance for your sins you are required to spend the next 20 years writing *very* politically correct press materials for Green Peace and PETA."

Leaving the judgment hall to begin their sentences, they notice Bill Gates in the adjoining hall handcuffed to Jennifer Lopez. As they are about to ask the docent what's going on they hear the familiar voice boom, "Jennifer Lopez, in penance for your sins...."

An architect with the incredibly bad judgment to use a Macintosh during the design of Bill Gates' mansion on Lake Washington was summarily dismissed when his horrible, insensitive gaffe was discovered and the wrath of Gates fell upon him.

Professionally destroyed and unable to find any work in the Seattle area, the architect fell into a deep depression. One day, no longer able to contemplate the prospect of living in a design world completely dominated by Microsoft products, he took his own life.

The next thing he knew he had materialized at the Pearly Gates of Heaven where Saint Peter was waiting.

"Ah," said Saint Peter, checking his book, "You're that poor architect who suffered so at the hands of Bill Gates. Don't worry, you're now quite safe here in Heaven."

Still quivering, the poor architect responded, "This is wonderful! But what will happen to me if Bill Gates finds me here?"

Saint Peter let out a broad laugh: "AS IF! You remember what the Bible says about rich men getting into Heaven? The eye of a needle? Camels? No? Well, never mind. Anyway, his influence up here will be limited. We still use mainframes and we don't even have a T1 Internet connection yet - we're stuck with a bunch of 56K baud modems we got at a clearance sale at Fry's Electronics in Silicon Valley."

Then, just inside the Pearly Gates, the architect spotted a familiar looking figure. Fit to be tied, the poor architect cried out in dismay, "Look, it's him," stammered the architect, his unease rising, "You...you told me he'd never get into Heaven, but it's HIM."

Saint Peter turned around to see who the architect was talking about.

"Oh, no, my son, that's really God. He just likes to dress up and pretend He's Bill Gates."

Bill Gates, back in New York for one of his regular meetings with stock market analysts, is in the elevator on the way to his room. After the other passengers get off, he finds himself alone with a stunningly beautiful young blonde model dressed in a tight fitting, low cut red cocktail dress that leaves very little to the imagination.

"Mr. Gates," she says breathlessly, leaning in so he can smell her intoxicating perfume, "I recognize you from the newspapers. I think you are just so amazing. You're so rich and so powerful and so unbelievably sexy that I just want to stop the elevator and make love to you right here, right now."

"So," says Bill, "What's in it for me?"

✦ ✦ ✦

Bill Gates died and, much to everyone's surprise, went to Heaven. When he got there, he had to wait in the common reception area with literally millions of people milling about. It was almost three weeks until, finally, a staff member in a dark blue windbreaker with the word "STAFF" emblazoned across the back in large yellow letters approached him.

"Good Afternoon," said the staffer in a voice borne of the boredom that comes from working in any large bureaucracy. "I'm Jennifer, your Heaven induction coordinator. Please give me your full name, last name first."

"Gates, William, the third."

As the coordinator started searching though the sheaf of papers on her clipboard, looking for Bill's record Bill asked, "What's going on here? Why are all these people here? Where's Saint Peter? Where are the Pearly Gates?"

Ignoring the questions until she located Bill's records, the coordinator looked up in surprise.

"It says here that you were the founder of Microsoft. So you're *that* Bill Gates. Is that correct?"

"Yes."

"Well then, to answer your questions, it's a matter of geometric population growth. A few millennia ago when this whole Pearly Gates business got started, it was no big deal. Only a couple hundred people died every day and Saint Peter could handle it all by himself. Who would have believed people would take that remark about "Go forth and multiply" so seriously. Now, with over six billion people on earth, ten thousand people die every hour - that's over a quarter-million people a day. Do you think Saint Peter has the time to meet them all personally?"

Doing the math quickly in his head Bill replied, "I guess not."

"So to keep up with demand Peter had to develop an organization. Now, Peter is the CEO of Heavenly Gate, Inc. He and the board sit at headquarters and make policy. The actual inductions are delegated to field staff members like me." After looking though her paperwork some more the induction coordinator continued, "Good news. It looks like your paperwork is all in order. With a management background like yours you should end up with a great job assignment."

"Job assignment?" replied the startled Gates, "As in WORK!!!"

"Of course," replied the coordinator. "Did you think you'd get to spend the rest of eternity just sitting on your ass, playing a harp and drinking ambrosia? You wish! Heaven is a big operation and everybody has to pull their weight around here!" Finally, the coordinator completed the quintriplicate form. Bill signed the form at the bottom and was given the canary and blue copies.

"The yellow copy is yours. Go down the street to the induction center and give the blue copy to your occupation orientation specialist," said the induction coordinator over her shoulder as she headed off to process the next inductee.

Musing on how this was not at all what he had expected, Bill walked down the road until he came to the induction center. After a six hour wait he was summoned into the office.

"Hi. I'm Kevin your occupation orientation specialist," said the specialist as he shook Bill's hand and introduced himself. "Let's just see what we have here." After looking at Bill's induction form he continued, "Sorry about the wait but Heaven is centuries behind in developing a information technology infrastructure," Kevin explained. "As you've seen, we still do everything on paper. It can take us a week to just process you new inductees."

"I had to wait *three* weeks," interjected Bill.

"So you see what I mean. But you're going to get a chance to make a real improvement in the system. Because of your background, your job is going to be Managing Director of Heaven's new online data processing center. We're building the largest computing facility in creation. There will be millions of computers all over the universe connected by the real 'ether net' and a high speed optical fiber WAN to a back-end server nest with thousands of server CPUs. RAID backup, fully fault tolerant, scalable. The whole nine yards."

Bill could barely contain his excitement. "Wow! What a network!! What a great job!!! This really is Heaven!!!!"

Kevin continued, "We're just finishing construction and we'll be going online soon. Would you like to go see the center now?"

"You bet!" replied Bill.

They caught a shuttle and after a ten minute ride they arrived at Heaven's new data processing center. This was, indeed, a truly huge facility, a hundred times larger than the NASA vehicle assembly building at Cape Canaveral. Workers were crawling all over the facility laying miles of fiber optic cables connecting to the huge server nest - thousands of server computers in racks, arranged neatly row-by-row, ... Sun systems ... all running Linux software! Not a PC or a copy of NT Server in sight! Even worse, the galleries of user workstations around the center were all populated with Macintosh G-4's.

Not a single byte of Microsoft code in all of Heaven!

The thought of spending eternity using products that he had spent his whole career working to destroy was too much for Bill.

"What about PCs???" he cried out. "What about Word? What about Excel? What about Windows? Surely there must be some Microsoft products around here??"

"You're forgetting something," said Kevin.

"What's that?" asked Bill.

"This is Heaven. We need a computer system that's user friendly, that's reliable, that's, well, 'HEAVENLY' to use. But if you really are going to be the Managing Director we'd want you to be comfortable. Are you sure you'd want to build a data processing center based on PCs running Windows?"

"Absolutely," said Bill. "It's my dream system."

"Well, OK then...," said Kevin, shaking his head and pressing a big red button that had suddenly materialized out of nowhere, "But I'm afraid that to work on a Windows based network like that you're going to have to .... **GO TO HELL!**"

Bill Gates' personal philosophy about customer service: If you build it, they will come. The trick is to keep them coming back for the upgrades.

## Bill Gate's personal choices for the Microsoft company song:

10. "Carry That Weight"

9. "You Ain't Seen Nothin' Yet"

8. "Time Is On My Side"

7. "Both Sides Now"

6. "Money Can't Buy Me Love"

5. "Under My Thumb"

4. "I Gotta Be Me"

3. "I Can See Clearly Now"

2. "I Did It My Way"

1. "It's My Party and I'll Cry If I Want To"

✦ ✦ ✦

God, having reached the end of His patience with the human race, decides to send down His angels to destroy the earth. Wanting to give the people at least some opportunity to repent, He summons the Pope, George W. Bush and Bill Gates and informs them that the world will end at precisely 12:01 AM, GMT, two weeks from this day of notice.

The Pope immediately returned to the Vatican and summoned the college of Cardinals. "Well," said the Pope, "I've got some good news and some bad news. The good news is that we were right all along and there is, in fact, a God. The bad news is that He is really pissed off and the world is going to end at 12:01 AM, GMT, two weeks from today. Notify the faithful to repent and prepare."

George W. Bush immediately returned to Washington D.C. and summoned his cabinet. "Well," said W., "I've got some bad news and some good news. The bad news is that God is really pissed off and He is going to destroy the world at 12:01 AM, GMT, two weeks from today. The good news is that we won't have to finish hunting down Osama bin Laden. Tell Dick he can come out of the shelter."

Bill Gates immediately returned to Redmond and summoned his senior staff. "Well," said Bill, "I've got some good news, some really good news and some really great news. The good news is that God knows who I am and He thinks I'm one of the three most important people in the world. The really good news is that we're not going to have to worry about how to sell Windows XP to everybody who finally just got around to upgrading to Windows Millennium edition. The really great news is that we can quit worrying about what the Department of Justice is going to try next to screw up our plans to dominate the world."

Bill Gates' personal philosophy about sales and marketing: A ton of marketing beats a pound of innovation any day.

✦ ✦ ✦

## 10 things you're not likely to hear Bill Gates say in public:

10. "I see your point"

9. "Are you STUPID!! Of course the money matters!!!"

8. "You'd think Ralph Nader would have something better to do"

7. "Paul Allen doesn't have to put up with this crap. Maybe if I bought a couple sports teams..."

6. "Real estate prices are down...hmmm...this may be a good time to buy the rest of Maui"

5. "This house is <u>way</u> too big"

4. "I love it...God help me I love it so"

3. "Maybe I should take some time off"

2. "Jeez...I hope my new charitable foundation will get some of these clowns off my back"

1. "Damn, Windows is still slow!"

President George W. Bush and Bill Gates are giving a joint news briefing when right in the middle of a question from reporter John Markoff of the *New York Times* an asteroid strikes the podium and kills all three of them. Upon arriving in Heaven, they are ushered in front of God's golden throne to justify their lives.

"Well," says God to Markoff, "What have you done to justify entering Heaven?"

"I lived a good life and I tried to use my position at the *Times* to completely and accurately report on how computer technology was affecting the human race," replied Markoff.

"Fine," replies God. "You may enter Heaven. You're next, Bush. What's your story?"

"Well," replies Bush, "I was President of the United States. Even though I lost the popular vote I became the most popular President in history by lowering taxes, improving education and making the world a safer place by helping eradicate international terrorism - and I did all this while Democrats and the press made fun of my occasional errors in grammarification."

"Impressive," says God. "Come up here and sit beside me on my golden throne so that we can talk some more later. Now, what have you got to say for yourself, Gates?"

"I think...," replies Bill, after thinking a minute, "That you're sitting in my seat."

✦ ✦ ✦

While sailing his yacht solo in the Pacific, Bill Gates fell overboard off the coast of Hawaii. After paddling around for a while in the tropical water he was picked up by a young man in a small sail boat.

Safely on board, Bill expressed his gratitude, "Thanks for saving me. I'm Bill Gates, the world's richest man. Name a reward and it's yours."

Thinking for a minute, the young man replied, "I'd like to have a way cool funeral and afterwards a major party for all my friends."

Pondering the odd request, Bill asked for clarification, "A fancy funeral seems like a pretty random request for someone your age. Isn't there something else more appropriate that you want."

"Well," replied the young man, "It's just that Steve Case, Chairman of AOL, is my uncle and when he finds out that I saved you from drowning he's going to kill me!!"

Bill Gates, Intellectual Ventures co-President CTO Nathan Myhrvold and physicist Stephen Hawking (Myhrvold's old mentor), were traveling across Scotland in a train. Bill looked out and noticed that in the middle of a herd of grazing sheep there was a single black sheep.

"That's interesting," said Bill, "I didn't know that there were black sheep in Scotland."

"Actually," corrected Myhrvold, always looking for a way to intellectually one up Bill, "All you can really say is that *one* sheep in Scotland is black. In fact, to be *accurate*, all you can really say is that one sheep in Scotland is black *on this side*."

"Actually," said Hawking, "To be *completely* accurate, all you can really say is that one sheep in Scotland is black on this side *some of the time*."

One afternoon the CEO of a struggling software developer locked in a bitter battle with Microsoft was taking a break to hike in the woods and regain his perspective. As he walked he happened upon an old brass lamp. Tarnished and covered with weeds, the lamp had clearly seen better days. As he sat down on a log and began polishing the lamp there was suddenly a bright blue flash and a small, rotund genie bearing an uncanny resemblance to PC industry guru John C. Dvorak popped into view amid a swirl of acrid smoke.

"I am the genie of the lamp," said the genie, "And I am here to grant you three wishes. You must choose now. Know ye, however, that this lamp was once the property of Bill Gates. Whatsoever you ask I am obligated to grant him two fold."

After thinking for a few minutes, the CEO responded, "For my first wish I want one billion dollars in my personal checking account."

"Your wish is my command. One billion dollars has been deposited in your personal checking account. Two billion dollars has also been deposited in Bill Gates's personal checking account."

"For my second wish," continued the CEO, "When I arrive home I want the woman of my dreams to be waiting for me."

"Your wish is my command. The woman of your dreams is awaiting your pleasure at your home. Two women of his dreams now await Bill Gates's pleasure."

"For my third and final wish," said the CEO, "I want you to listen <u>very</u> closely. I'm going to go from here to the nearest hospital. Once I'm safely there, I want to have a heart attack that exactly half kills me."

"Your wish is my command," replied the genie.

According to the "Bill Gates Net Worth Page" (web address: www.quuxuum.org/~evan/bgnw.html), as of January 2002 Bill's Microsoft stock alone (and ignoring all his other investments) was worth about $41 *billion* dollars. Even with no interest, dividends or stock price increase, at $1,000,000 per day it would still take him about 112 years to spend it all. And that's no joke!!

✦ ✦ ✦

## 4.0 Windows

Proof positive that Windows, in all its various incarnations, is really not a virus. While it is true that both viruses and Windows:

- Replicate quickly
- Use up valuable host system resources
- Slow the host system down
- Occasionally trash the host system hard disk
- Hide unknown to the user among host system programs
- Mimic a variety of system problems

There are still fundamental differences: Viruses are fast, compact, efficient, machine independent, stealthy, robust and stable. Since this is clearly not true of Windows, Windows cannot be virus. It is more accurately a *plague*.

The Microsoft Windows development team and members of the Open Source Initiative decided to have a rowing race on lake Washington. Agreeing on eight man sculls, both teams practiced hard and by race day they were as ready as they could be. Unfortunately, to the chagrin of many, the Microsoft team won by a mile.

Afterwards, the Open Source team members were very depressed and they decided that the reason for their crushing defeat had to be found. After much discussion, a work group from sales, marketing, software engineering and technical support was set up to investigate and report back. After three months of research and investigation they came up with the answer and the work group coordinator gave the summary presentation to the assembled Open Source members.

"To be brief," he said, "The problem was that Microsoft had eight people rowing and one person steering. We, on the other hand, had one person rowing and eight people steering."

Excited that the problem was now understood, the work group was then asked to go away and come up with a plan so that Open Source could win the following year's race and assuage their damaged pride.

Two months later, the work group had worked out a detailed plan, and the coordinator gave his short summary to the excited Open Source members:

"Basically, the person rowing the boat has got to work harder."

Three friends were out for a summer drive: a mechanical engineer, an electronics engineer and a Microsoft Windows developer. Suddenly, without warning, the engine stopped and the car coasted to a stop by the roadside.

After examining the car carefully the mechanical engineer said, "Looks to me like a fuel system problem - probably a clogged fuel injector. I'll fix it and we'll be on our way."

The electronics engineer disagreed, "No way!! I think it's an electrical system problem - probably the electronic ignition. I'll fix it and we'll be on our way."

The Windows developer shook his head and said, "Hey guys, before you do any of that stuff I have a much simpler idea: let's just close all the windows then turn the ignition key 'off'. If we wait a minute or two we should be able to restart it and everything ought to run fine again!"

Q.    How do you keep a Windows developer from drowning?

A.    Shoot him before he hits the water.

## 10 Least requested new features for Windows XP:

10. Dial up networking interface for home shopping network

9. Hard disk re-fragmenter

8. Blue screen of death banner ads

7. Add playing, "You Lose . . . Ha, Ha, Ha" WAV file to General Protection Fault (GPF) processing

6. Device driver for veg-o-matic

5. Registry randomizer

4. Linux compatibility box

3. Vibrator Plug n' Play interface

2. Make changing items on the Start Up menu even more confusing

1. The new "ET phone home" user registration system

## SECRET MICROSOFT WINDOWS AD MESSAGE?

A television ad by Microsoft featured theme music from the Confutatis of Mozart's D minor Requiem, K.626. While the happy users cavort and gambol on the screen and the tag line "Where do you want to go today?" is prominently featured, in the background the chorus is singing:

> Confutatis maledictis,
> flammis acribus addictis,
> Voca me cum benedictus.
>
> Oro supplex et acclinis,
> cor contritum quasi cinis
> Gere curam mei finis.

which roughly translates to:

> While the wicked are confounded,
> Doomed to flames without bounds,
> Summon me with your blessing.
>
> Low I kneel and bow in submission.
> My heart, like ashes, in contrition;
> Attend me at my death.

Maybe there's a message here?

An attractive woman was confiding in one of her girl friends that even though she had been married three times the marriages had never been consummated.

"What about your first husband?" asked the friend.

"Well, it turned out that he was gay so he wouldn't."

"And what about your second husband?" continued the friend.

"Well, he was injured in the Gulf war so he couldn't."

"And what about your current husband?" continued the bemused friend.

"Well, he's a Microsoft Windows system programmer working on the new Windows.NET Server operating system and if he gets home at all, all he can do is talk about how big it is and how insanely great it is going to be when I get it."

In an interview with the Chicago Sun-Times published on June 1, 2001, Steve Ballmer characterized, "Linux is a Cancer".

Wrong. According to Linus Torvalds, while the exact birthdate of Linux is unknown, after some initial development Torvalds says, "I'd guess the first version {0.01}went out in the middle of September 1991." Clearly this means that Linux is a Virgo (August 23 - September 22). (**Ed. Note:** Linus Torvalds is the original developer of Linux.)

Windows XP, on the other hand, was officially launched by Microsoft on October 25, 2001. That means that Windows XP is a Scorpio (October 24 - November 21) and we all know how much fun scorpions are to work and play with!!

Sign on a Microsoft Windows development group's office wall:

> **Remember: Any sufficiently advanced software is indistinguishable from a rigged demo.**

TOTALLY
## The Unauthorized Microsoft Joke Book - 2nd Edition

**Q.**  What do you call a UPS truck loaded with 10,000 copies of Windows XP driving off the floating bridge into Lake Washington?

**A.**  A good start.

✦ ✦ ✦

If cars ran on Microsoft Windows (and watch out, because with the continued expansion of Windows CE into dedicated applications they are bound to try it eventually!) here are some unique features of your new WinCar :

1.  Regularly, performing some routine driving maneuver would cause your WinCAR to stop on the road. You would be expected to accept this, restart the car and drive on without complaints.

2.  Occasionally, your WinCAR would just stop on the road for no reason at all. You would be expected to accept this, too, restart the car and drive on without complaints.

3.  Rarely, your WinCAR would just stop on the road for no reason at all, destroying its engine, transmission and drive train in the process and requiring you to install a complete set of new parts. Incredibly, you would be expected to accept this, too, repair the car at your own expense and resume driving without complaints.

4.  In your WinCAR the normal automobile instruments for oil pressure, water temperature, fuel level, electrical system status, etc. would all be replaced by a single "General Vehicle Fault" blue indicator light. This "blue bulb of death" indicator would come on just after one of the failures described in 1, 2 or 3 has occurred and it is now too late for you to do anything about it.

5.  You could not take any passengers with you in your WinCAR unless you bought an extra cost "multi-user" option for each additional passenger seat.

6.    Your WinCAR would only run using Microsoft gas, oil and lubricating fluids.

7.    In a collision, your WinCAR's airbag system would require you to click on "Continue?" before deploying.

8.    Your WinCAR would have a special sound system which unfortunately would only be able to receive Microsoft FM radio stations and play Microsoft cassettes or CDs.

9.    Every two years you would be forced to upgrade to a new version of WinCAR with many exciting "new" features that have been available on other cars for years. After upgrading your WinCAR many accessories purchased from other vendors would never run the same again.

10.    Every new model of your WinCAR would require a larger engine to equal the performance of the last model.

Of course, related to the new Microsoft WinCAR are the new Microsoft tires - they not only stop on a dime, they pick it up!!!

**Q.**    How many Microsoft Windows software developers does it take to write a clean, efficient, multi-tasking operating system?

**A.**    More

**Q.**    What do you call 25 skydiving Microsoft Windows software developers falling through the sky?

**A.**    Skeet

# 10 Windows applications you are not likely to see from Microsoft:

10. WinScope - personal horoscope generator

9. WinDog - pari-mutuel dog race handicapper

8. WinDOW - stock market modeler

7. WinDigestable - restaurant guide

6. WinGaffe - automatic politically incorrect comment generator

5. WinCandescent - light bulb usable life calculator

4. WinCest - sex game for the whole family

3. WinCommunicable - virus distribution utility (to replace Outlook)

2. WinCarnation - next life planner

1. WinWin - negotiation strategy planner

# The Windows GPF (General Protection Fault) song (sung to "Jingle Bells")

GPF, GPF, GPF today
Oh, what fun it is to try to crash just once a day!!!
GPF, GPF, GPF today
Oh, what fun it is to try to crash just once a day!!!

Booting once again
Trying to stay calm
The files are blown away
The drivers are all gone!!!

Norton doesn't help.
The registry I'll hack.
Instead of trusting Microsoft
I should have bought a Mac.

<chorus>

It says my memory's bad
And that I should buy more.
For what I've spent to date
I could have bought a car.

The damn thing still won't load
My work remains undone.
If Gates were here I swear
I would be reaching for a gun.

<chorus>

It ate my data base
And all my open files.
And then when I reboot
The damn thing is all smiles.

I'm at my patience' end.
I don't know what to do.
The only thing I know for sure
Is soon it will screw YOU.

<chorus>

## MICROSOFT SET TO SELL ADS IN ERROR MESSAGES

REDMOND, WASHINGTON (AP) -- Microsoft today announced that will begin selling advertising space in the error messages that appear in Windows XP. Pointing out that the typical user of Windows unavoidably encounters numerous error messages every day, Microsoft has decided to take advantage of these opportunities to display advertising messages. While initially to be limited to Microsoft products, Microsoft stated that they expect to ultimately sell space with pricing based upon the specific error message and the frequency with which that error message is displayed.

"We estimate that throughout the world at any given moment several million people are staring at a 'General Protection Fault', 'Illegal Operation' or any of a number of other Windows error messages or warnings," stated a Microsoft spokesperson. "We will be able to generate significant revenue by including a short advertising message along with them." Also under consideration at Microsoft are plans to add banner ads to the terminate and stay dead "Blue Screen of Death".

The United States Department of Justice reacted to the Microsoft announcement by indicating that they intend to immediately investigate whether Microsoft is gaining an unfair advantage in reaching the public with this advertising by virtue of its semi-monopolistic control over Windows error messages.

**Q.** What is the definition of "multi-tasking" in Windows?

**A.** When two or more users are staring at the hourglass wait cursor on the same computer at the same time.

Scientists at the United States Centers for Disease Control in Atlanta today confirmed that the viruses which cause the dreaded English strains of hoof and mouth disease and of mad cow disease cannot be spread by Microsoft's Outlook Windows email application. This is believed to be the first time that Outlook has ever failed to propagate a major virus.

"Frankly, we've never heard of a virus that couldn't be spread via Microsoft Outlook," said a spokesperson from the CDC's infectious disease unit, "So our findings were, to say the least, unexpected."

The study was immediately hailed by British health officials, who said it will save millions of pounds and thousands of man hours. "Up until now we have, quite naturally, assumed that both hoof and mouth and mad cow were being spread by Microsoft Outlook," said a spokesman for Britain's Agriculture Ministry. "By eliminating Outlook as a source of infection we can focus our resources elsewhere."

Executives at Microsoft, meanwhile, were skeptical, insisting that Outlook's proprietary Virus Propagation Protocol (VPP) has proven virtually unimpervious to any virus. The company, however, announced that it will issue a free VPP patch to anyone requesting it if it turns out that Outlook is, in fact, not able to successfully propagate the hoof and mouth or mad cow viruses.

The Centers for Disease control also confirmed that they were still testing Outlook for its ability to propagate the Ebola Zaire, smallpox and HIV viruses. The results of these virus propagation tests will be announced as they are confirmed.

## Windows Crash Haikus

Continue? Or Not.
Machine demands I reply.
Either way I lose.

Cryptic message now
warns of impending doom.
I cringe in advance.

An error announced.
No clues. No hints. No warnings.
Screen. Mind. All are blank.

The blue screen returns.
Strange sounds from inside the case.
No good comes of this.

My call to Windows
support answered at last. I
still hear the laughter.

It looks so peaceful
with nothing on the blue screen.
Turn the power off.

A spreadsheet that big
may have held important truths.
It is gone forever.

A week of work gone.
It was there. Now it is not.
My scream goes unheard.

## 5.0   Microsoft Product Development and Support

**Q.**   What's the difference between any Microsoft 1.0 product release and a virus?

**A.**   With the virus, updates are free (and the documentation is usually better!)

"Where did you get that great motorcycle?" the Microsoft programmer asked as his friend pulled up on a brand new motorcycle.

"I was just sitting on the campus having a soda," the friend replied, "When this gorgeous blonde rode up, screeched to a stop and hopped off. She threw the motorcycle on the ground, stripped off her clothes and screamed, "OK, big boy, take what you want RIGHT NOW!!!"

"Good choice," replied his friend in obvious agreement, "The clothes would probably have been too small."

A pilot in a small airplane is lost in the fog somewhere over northwest Washington. He calls approach control at SeaTac but they are unable to locate him on radar. Almost out of fuel, he tentatively descends lower and lower looking for a landmark. Finally, he spots the gray outline of a building below and, as luck would have it, there is a person up on the roof. Shouting to be heard over the engine he yells down to the person, "Where am I??" to which the person on the roof immediately replies, "You're in an airplane!"

Triumphant, he immediately contacts SeaTac for a vector from 47°40'27" N, 122°7'13" W to the airport.

"If you're so lost, how do you know your current position with such precision?" queried the skeptical SeaTac airport approach controller.

"I'm over the Microsoft campus, above the technical support center," replied the now confident pilot. "It's the only place in the local area where you can get a response that is both completely accurate and totally useless!!!"

On the new product front, it's rumored that Microsoft has developed a new, compact ergonomic chair for use by programmers. Dubbed the "Microsoft Stool," beta testers have not been impressed with early evaluation copies of the retail packaged versions. "After all," said one reviewer on the condition of anonymity, "We've received shrink wrapped stool samples from Microsoft before."

### Haikus to a Microsoft Office upgrade

Another MS Office
upgrade announced this day.
my wallet winces.

MS Office grows
to take yet more space on disk.
I question the need.

Upgrading takes time.
The blue bar moves unbidden.
My foreboding grows.

Installed at long last
Office upgrade now complete.
Nothing works as before.

## 10 Design objectives missing from most Microsoft new products:

10. Has all the features that were announced

9. Appears stable on all current platforms

8. Done on time

7. Fully install in less than 100M of hard disk space

6. Runs without requiring additional memory

5. Completely usable without upgrading Windows version

4. Can ship on less than six CD ROMs

3. Runs much faster than originally anticipated

2. Appears to be fully compatible with non-Microsoft applications

1. Too perfect - won't need to sell a bug-fix upgrade for years

**10 Microsoft products that <u>didn't</u> change the world (these were real!!):**

10.  DOS Cobol compiler

9.  Mach 20 PC Accelerator

8.  Windows 1.x

7.  Windows 2.x

6.  Windows 386

5.  Pen Windows

4.  Xenix

3.  Multiplan

2.  OS/2

1.  BOB

✦ ✦ ✦

# MICROSOFT NEW PRODUCT HYPE DECODER

| What They Say | What It Means |
|---|---|
| ALL NEW | Not compatible with last release |
| UNMATCHED PERFORMANCE | Works almost as well as competitive products |
| TRUE MULTI-TASKING | Can crash several programs at once |
| INTUITIVE INTERFACE | Operation is completely illogical |
| NEW, IMPROVED | You wouldn't pay if we said we just fixed all the bugs from the last release |
| FOOLPROOF INSTALLATION | If you install it, it's proof you're a fool |
| ADVANCED DESIGN | Even the PR agency doesn't have a clue what this software is good for |
| FIELD PROVEN | We're still fixing the bugs reported from the last release |
| EXCELLENT REVIEWS | We bought a lot of advertising |
| YEARS IN DEVELOPMENT | It finally works well enough that you might actually pay money for it |

| | |
|---|---|
| **REVOLUTIONARY** | Completely incompatible with existing standards |
| **BREAKTHROUGH** | Nobody really needs this now |
| **NEW TECHNOLOGY** | The old technology didn't work at all |
| **UNPRECEDENTED FEATURES** | Does things even we can't explain |
| **SATISFACTION GUARANTEED** | Ours, not yours. If you buy this turkey, we're satisfied |

**Q.** What do you call a Microsoft technical support representative who can answer 20% of the incoming customer questions?

**A.** An overachiever.

The wife of a Microsoft technical support engineer went to the doctor to ask his help in reviving her man's sex drive. "What about trying Viagra?" asked the doctor.

"No way," replied the distraught wife. "I can't even get him to take an aspirin for a headache."

"No problem. Grind the pill up and put the powder into his coffee; he won't even taste it. Try it and come back in a week to let me know how it worked."

A week later the wife returned and the doctor inquired as to the results. "Oh, it was horrible, just terrible, doctor," cried the wife, bursting into tears.

"What happened?"

"Well, I did just as you advised," she replied. "I ground up the pill and slipped the powder into his coffee just like you suggested. After about ten minutes the effect was amazing. He jumped up from the chair, swept off the table, ripped my clothes off and then proceeded to make mad, passionate love to me right there on the tabletop. It was terrible!!"

"What was so terrible about that? I thought you wanted a more exciting sex life."

"Oh, no doctor, don't misunderstand. The sex was the best we've had in 15 years, but I'll never be able to show my face at that McDonald's again."

**Q.**  Why do they bury Microsoft software developers at least 20 feet under ground?

**A.**  Deep down they are really good people.

Note on the bulletin board in a Microsoft development group:

**Programming here is like sex: one mistake with a release and you may have to support it for a lifetime.**

## Microsoft CONFIDENTIAL:

## Top Secret Internal Software Development Process

1. Order T-shirts for development team.
2. Pre-announce product to press.
3. Announce unrealistic ship date.
4. Denounce anything competitive and currently shipping as old, outmoded and obsolete.
5. Denounce anything competitive and not currently shipping as unproven, untested vaporware.
6. Write program.
7. Write manual and specifications. (Writing these after programming helps the software match more closely.)
8. Assign product marketing team.
9. Write reviews for press.
10. Announce real ship date.
11. Rent famous venue for launch event.
12. Hire celebrity.
13. License rock song.
14. Stage launch event.
15. Ship product.
16. Test (early users provide lots of help here).
17. Identify bugs. Separate into features, real problems and potential enhancements.
18. Announce the upgrade program.

A Microsoft technical writer dies and arrives in Hell, where Satan growls, "Wait here while I drop these other sinners into the pit! Feel free to look around. When I come back you'll have to chose a room in which to spend all of eternity."

After Satan leaves the terrified writer gets up and peeks behind a door with the number "ONE" painted on it in blood and sees technical writers knee deep in boiling oil agonizingly trying to organize millions of lines of new product documentation on old PC's with small screens, broken keyboards and WordPerfect 5.0.

Horrified, the writer moves down the hall and peeks behind a door with a big red "TWO" on it, only to see another group of technical writers attempting to organize huge piles of new product screen shots while being scratched and bitten by a pack of small, porcine demons with razor sharp teeth and claws.

Barely able to contain his terror, the writer moves further down the hall and with trepidation peeks behind a door with no number. To his surprise, he sees a technical writer seated in a luxurious leather chair at the head of a polished conference table. Even stranger, he's surrounded by a bevy of fawning Microsoft software developers who are offering him a variety of cigars, snacks, and fine wines while hanging on his every word and telling him how his valuable insight and documentation genius is going to make this a much better Microsoft product.

At last, Satan returns and asks, "OK, times up. Choose. Which door will it be?"

The technical writer quickly pointed to the unnumbered door.

"You can't have that door," replied Satan with a snort. "That's part of Microsoft software developer Hell."

**10 Lines from Microsoft Technical Support that tell you it's a BIG problem:**

10. "Just download the patch from our web page."

9. "You probably just need to reinstall Windows from the distribution CD."

8. "WOAH!!! I've never heard of it doing THAT before."

7. "I hope you had your system backed up before you started this."

6. "Sounds like a hardware problem to me."

5. "Hmmm........ It really shouldn't do that."

4. "This system isn't in a mission critical application, is it?"

3. "I'll call you back later if I find anything out."

2. "I hope you kept all the original packing materials."

1. "Can you reach the plug?"

✦ ✦ ✦

A Microsoft technical support engineer dies and upon arriving at the Pearly Gates is informed by Saint Peter that he must spend 10 years in purgatory before he will be allowed into Heaven. However, he does get to choose between Microsoft software design purgatory and Microsoft technical support purgatory.

"What's the difference?" asked the curious techie.

"Well," replied Saint Peter, "In software design Purgatory each day demons tie you to a stake, soak you in gasoline, light you on fire with a match and you burn for the next 12 hours. Then you get to rest for the next 12 hours. In technical support purgatory you wait around for 12 hours for the software designers to burn then the demons tie you to a stake, soak you in gasoline, light you on fire with a match and you burn for the next 12 hours."

"Doesn't sound like much of a difference," replied the skeptical technoid.

"If I were you," counseled Saint Peter, "I'd take software design purgatory. The ropes tend to break, the stake is easy to pull out of the ground and somebody usually forgets the gasoline or the matches."

A beginning balloonist was up on his first solo flight. Unfortunately, when the wind veered he was blown off course and forced to land out in the country. He found himself in an open field with no idea of where he was. Fortunately, a car was coming down a nearby road and he flagged it down. The balloonist asked the driver, "Can you please tell me where I am?"

"Yes, of course", said the driver. "It's obvious that this wind has blown your balloon off course. You have just landed in the south field on a private farm owned by the Miller family. The farm is 16.25 miles from Redmond, Washington and it is 112.5 acres in total size. The Millers will be plowing this field next week and planting winter wheat. Also, there is a very aggressive bull in the field and he is charging you RIGHT NOW!!"

Just at that moment the bull lunged and flipped the balloonist over the fence. Fortunately, while a little banged up he was not seriously hurt. He got up, dusted himself off and asked the driver, "So, how long have you been a Microsoft technical support specialist?"

"That's amazing!!" said the driver, taken aback, "You're right. I do work in technical support at Microsoft. How did you know that?"

"I deal with Microsoft technical support all the time," replied the balloonist. "The information you gave me was detailed, precise and accurate. Most of it was useless or redundant and by the time you got to the critical information it was too late to be of any help."

"So, how long have you been in management?" retorted the technical support specialist.

Now it was the balloonist's turn to be surprised. "Unbelievable!! I am a senior manager. How could you possibly know that?"

"Because you didn't know where you were going, you don't know where you are and you expect me to be able to help! Plus, you're still just as lost as you were before we met but now you think it's all my fault!"

✦ ✦ ✦

**Q.**   What's a good weight for a Microsoft software developer?

**A.**   About 12 pounds, including the urn.

✦ ✦ ✦

Returning from a computer industry trade show the coach cabin for the flight was overbooked so the Microsoft technical support engineer got a free upgrade to first class. During the flight the first class passengers were given a gourmet meal with big, warm fudge brownies for desert. Too full to eat another bite, the technical support guy decided to save the brownies for later and, not having anything handy in which to wrap them, placed them in the motion sickness bag from the seat pocket in front of him.

After the plane landed, when he got up to leave carrying the bag, a stewardess approached.

"Sir," she asked, "Would you like for me to dispose of that for you?"

"No thanks," replied the engineer, "I'm saving it for my kids."

Of course, then there was the Microsoft technical support person who was overheard telling a customer, "You need to be really careful not to get locked into Open Systems."

**Q.** What makes Microsoft technical support engineers such great lovers?

**A.** They always know when <u>not</u> to answer the telephone!!

A Microsoft software engineer had been missing from work for over a week when someone finally noticed his empty office. After several calls to his home went unreturned his supervisor became concerned and called the police. When they arrived at his apartment and pounded on the door there was no answer so they broke through the door but alas, found him dead in the shower, water still running, an empty bottle of organic shampoo next to his shriveled body.

What had happened? Was it foul play? Natural causes? Suicide? Who was to blame? The mystery was finally solved, when one of his fellow engineers picked up the shampoo bottle and read the instructions:

> Wet hair
> Apply shampoo to hair
> Lather
> Rinse hair thoroughly
> Repeat

**10 Signs your Microsoft technical support person has completely lost it:**

10. Responds "Hah! Wouldn't you like to know?" to all questions.

9. Attempts to mind meld with your Pentium chip over the phone. Succeeds.

8. Keeps asking you if this is a test.

7. Suggests you call an exorcist immediately.

6. Tells you to perform a "quick uninstall" by waving a really large magnet over your hard disk.

5. Threatens to cast a spell on you if you don't follow his exact instructions.

4. Recommends chicken soup, lots of fluids and plenty of rest to get rid of a computer virus.

3. You realize the drooling you're hearing is not coming from a pet bulldog.

2. Brags about creating seven of the top ten computer viruses.

1. Asks every caller, "Do you know how long it's been since I've had a date?"

✦ ✦ ✦

## 6.0 Big, Bad Bill, Part II

Bill Gates dies and finds himself at the Pearly Gates. Meeting him, Saint Peter informs Bill that due to his celebrity status he will be allowed to choose between an eternity in Heaven or Hell. Gates, dead but no fool, asks if he can look around both places before making his decision.

"Very well," says St. Peter. " Let's start with Hell."

There is immediately a flash and they are transported to the nether regions. When the smoke clears Bill is surprised to see beautiful beaches. A marimba band is playing in the background. There are gorgeous women in revealing swimsuits. A great buffet is laid out. The place has all the trappings of a world class resort.

"Very impressive," enthuses Gates, figuring that if this is Hell, the downside of being dead must be pretty limited. "Let's check out Heaven, now."

Another flash and they are transported back to the ethereal plane. A soft white light glows everywhere. There are discussion groups debating various aspects of theology. A heavenly choir singing joyous praises to God is heard continuously. Everyone is wearing comfortable unisex leisure suits. It looks and sounds like Oral Roberts University.

"No offense," says Bill after a moment of thought, "But based upon what I've seen I think I'll take Hell."

There is a final flash and Bill is stunned to find himself chained hip deep in a pool of molten lava with his skin being flayed off by a trio of horrible looking dwarves whose uncanny resemblance's to Gary Kildall, Jerry Kaplan and Ray Noorda are striking.

When Bill screams in pain for help, a Window opens and a Videotext image of Saint Peter appears.

"What's the problem?" asks Saint Peter.

**"WHAT'S THE PROBLEM!!!"** shrieks Bill. **"THIS ISN'T WHAT YOU SHOWED ME. WHERE IS THE POOL, THE BEACH, THE BUFFET, THE BABES????"**

"Ah," smiled Saint Peter, "Before you were just looking at the demo. This is the REAL Hell, Release 6.66"

**Ed. Note**: or, if you prefer, an alternative ending:

"Ah," smiled Saint Peter, "Before you were just a tourist. Now you're a resident."

✦ ✦ ✦

President George W. Bush, Bill Gates, the Dali Lhama and a deadheading Microsoft systems programmer are all flying back to Seattle on the Microsoft corporate jet when the pilot sprints through the cabin, yells, "The plane is out of control...grab a parachute and jump for your lives," grabs a parachute, heaves open the emergency exit door and jumps out. Unfortunately, since the programmer is an unscheduled passenger they are one parachute short.

President Bush jumps up, proclaims, "I'm President of the United States and the world needs me and my experience to defeat international terrorism." He grabs a parachute and jumps.

Bill Gates jumps up, proclaims, "I'm the richest, smartest man in the world and the future of world technology will be in chaos without me. Besides, it's my plane." He grabs a parachute and jumps.

The Dali Lhama and the programmer look at each other for a minute then the Dali Lhama proclaims, "Go ahead, my son, save yourself. Life is transcendant and I fear not death. I'll be back. Your whole life is ahead of you. Please take the last parachute and jump."

"It's cool," replies the programmer. "We can both jump. The richest, smartest man in the world just jumped with my new, extra-large, 24-pocket laptop computer carrying case."

✦ ✦ ✦

Bill Gates decides to throw a massive party for his fiftieth birthday. During the party he grabs the microphone and announces to his guests that down in the garden of his famous Lake Washington mansion he has had the swimming pool stocked with two great white sharks and a couple hundred piranhas. "I will give anything they desire to any person who has the courage to swim across that pool."

There are no takers so the party continues for a couple hours until suddenly there is a great splash down by the pool. When all the guests run to poolside to find out what has happened they see Larry Ellison (who had secretly crashed the party) swimming as hard as he can for the far side of the pool. Fins are flashing, jaws are snapping and the water is frothing but Larry just keeps on going. Just as the sharks are about to overtake him he reaches the far side of the pool and clambers out; tired and wet, with a few piranhas hanging off him he is otherwise unharmed.

Overwhelmed by this demonstration of skill and courage, Bill again grabs the microphone and says, "I am a man of my word. Larry, even though we have been fierce competitors I will give you anything, absolutely anything, you name for you are undoubtedly the bravest man I have ever seen."

Ellison grabs the microphone out of Bill's hand and yells, "Why don't we start by finding Steve Ballmer. He's the one who shoved me in!"

Bill Gates and two senior Microsoft development managers went out to lunch. While walking back by some new construction on the Microsoft campus they saw a dirty, dented brass lamp lying next to a recently dug trench. Curious, one of the managers picked it up and gave it a rub. Instantly, a genie appeared.

"You know the drill," said the genie, "Three wishes. But since there are three of you, I'm going to only give you one wish each."

"Great!!" said the first manager. "Send me to Hawaii forever with a beautiful blonde."

POOF!! There was a bright flash of light, a puff of blue smoke and he was gone.

"Now me, Now me!!" said the excited second manager. "Send me to Tahiti forever with two beautiful blondes."

POOF!! As before, there was a bright flash of light, a puff of blue smoke and he was gone.

The genie then turned to Bill Gates. "And now, what do you want?"

Thinking a minute, Bill smiled, "I want those two back in their offices and working at their desks right now."

Of course, it's not all about the money for Bill. We heard that he skipped the novocaine during a root canal because he wanted to transcend dental medication.

Bill Gates awoke in a hospital bed after major surgery and found that the curtains in his hospital room were tightly drawn, darkening the room.

"Why are the curtains closed?" he asked the nurse.

The nurse replied, "There's a huge fire burning out of control in the building right across the street from your window. We were afraid that you might wake up, see all the smoke and flames and think that the operation was unsuccessful."

Bill Gates' personal philosophy about innovation in new product development: The early bird may get the worm but the second mouse gets the cheese.

♦ ♦ ♦

# 10 Things not to tell Bill Gates at the staff meeting:

10. "Heard any good jokes, lately?"

9. "Where would you like this box of subpoenas?"

8. "The new Office Pro retail package is so heavy it ruptured a beta tester."

7. "Hackers replaced our Internet home page with a link to 'Surf Nazis from Hell'."

6. "Mike Wallace is in the lobby."

5. "The CD duplicators screwed up and sent us 2,500,000 copies of 'Salty Dog's Select XXX JPEG Collection' instead of the production run of Windows XP CDs."

4. "The XXX JPEG collection is already up to number 7 on our best seller list and outselling Windows XP upgrades by over 25 to 1."

3. "Quit rocking, you're making me dizzy!"

2. "John Ashcroft is calling on line 2."

1. "Your wife's lawyer is calling on line 1."

Bill Gates' personal philosophy of business: When you've got them by the balls, their hearts and minds will follow.

✦ ✦ ✦

While driving home from the Microsoft company Christmas party, Bill and his wife were pulled over by a Washington State Trooper. After examining his driver's license and registration, the officer said to Bill, "Mr. Gates, do you realize that you were going over 70 mph in a 45 mph zone?"

"No way," replied Bill. "I can barely get over 60 in this damn diesel."

"Hah," said Melinda, unbidden. "My husband is a notorious speed demon. Everybody knows it. I think we were going over 80!"

Bill glares at her but keeps his cool.

"Also," continued the trooper, "Mr. Gates, I notice that you are not wearing your seat belt. That's an infraction here in Washington and I'm going to have to write you a ticket for that, too."

"Now wait a minute," said Bill, becoming a bit more agitated. "I just unbuckled the seat belt when you pulled us over so I could get out my wallet."

"What a liar," said Melinda. "He never wears his seat belt. I nag him about it all the time."

**"GOD DAMN IT, MELINDA,"** yelled Bill, losing it. **"WILL YOU JUST SHUT UP AND LET ME HANDLE THIS!!!!"**

"Excuse me, Mrs. Gates," interrupted the trooper. "Is Mr. Gates always this verbally abusive to you?"

"Why no, officer," replied Melinda with a wicked smile, "Only when he drinks."

✦ ✦ ✦

## 10 Things about himself Bill Gates would rather you did NOT know:

10. Secretly watches every episode of *Buffy the Vampire Slayer*.

9. Has complete collection of Fantastic Four comics. Likes to pretend he's Reed Richards.

8. Had sand kicked in his face at the beach. Last year. By Larry Ellison.

7. Major case of athletes foot.

6. Tried to rent the Vatican for Windows XP launch.

5. Knocked himself out when working out with Taebo tapes.

4. Owns a private island retreat. Australia.

3. Uses AOL promotional CD's as pooper scoopers when walking dog.

2. Like to dress up like Darth Vader.

1. Has no will. Plans to take it with him.

Bill Gates, director Francis Ford Coppola and Loudcloud CEO Marc Andreeson are captured by cannibals on a remote pacific island. Asked by the chief of the tribe for one last request before he has them boiled for lunch, Francis Ford Coppola thinks for a moment then said, "I'd like to see a final screening of *Citizen Kane*, the greatest movie ever made."

The chief, while personally preferring *Eating Raoul*, agrees.

Bill Gates, when asked for his last request, responds, "Since the screen is already set up I'd like to give the tribe a complete multimedia presentation as to why Windows XP Professional with high level browser integration represents the <u>true</u> future of access to the Internet. I consider it Microsoft's crowning achievement and even if I'm gone you will eventually need this information."

Not sure what it all means, the chief nonetheless agrees, but before they can get started, Andreeson, blurted out his request: "For God's sake please boil me before Bill's presentation."

After losing $26 billion or so in a vicious bear stock market correction, Bill Gates asked his wife, "Melinda, if I lost all of my money and all of my power would you still love me?"

"Of course I would," replied Melinda sweetly, "and I'd *miss* you, too."

Sign on Bill Gate's wall:

**The race is between Microsoft's efforts to develop idiot-proof software and the Universe's efforts to produce bigger idiots.**

Sign on Microsoft software development group wall:

**So far, the Universe is winning.**

Scott McNealy decided to call Bill Gates to see if Sun and Microsoft could work out their differences. Calling Bill's direct line, Scott said, "Is Bill there? This is Scott McNealy from Sun Microsystems."

After a long pause, Gates's private secretary responded with sorrow in her voice, "I'm sorry, Mr. McNealy, but while there has been no public announcement yet, Mr. Gates passed away suddenly yesterday."

Ten minutes later, he called again, "Is Bill there? This is Scott McNealy from Sun Microsystems."

"As I told you earlier, Mr. McNealy," said the secretary, "Mr. Gates passed away yesterday."

Ten minutes later, he called again, "Is Bill there? This is Scott McNealy from Sun Microsystems."

"**LISTEN YOU INSENSITIVE JERK,**" screamed the secretary, losing her cool, "**I'VE TOLD YOU TWICE ALREADY THAT MR. GATES IS DEAD. GONE. DECEASED. NOT LIVING. KICKED THE BUCKET. GONE TO THE GREAT PERHAPS. BOUGHT THE FARM. SHUFFLED OFF THIS MORTAL COIL. WHICH WORDS DON'T YOU UNDERSTAND AND WHY DO YOU KEEP CALLING BACK?**"

"Well," replied McNealy, "I just love to hear you say it."

On a foggy evening Bill Gates was sailing his yacht on the Puget Sound when he noticed the light of another ship directly ahead. Getting on the radio, Gates radioed, "Oncoming ship, please divert your course 10 degrees south to avoid a collision."

The response: "Acknowledged. We recommend you divert YOUR course 10 degrees north to avoid a collision."

Gates: "I have the right of way. I say again, divert **YOUR** course south to avoid a collision."

The response: "Acknowledged. We say again, we recommend you divert **YOUR** course north."

Gates was outraged: **"THIS IS BILL GATES SPEAKING AND I HAVE THE RIGHT OF WAY. I BRAKE FOR NOBODY. DIVERT YOUR COURSE SOUTH IMMEDIATELY TO AVOID A COLLISION!"**

The response: "Acknowledged. This is the Port Orchard lighthouse. Your choice."

✦ ✦ ✦

Bill Gates had just finished a particularly intense courtroom session in his long running anti-trust battle with the U.S. Department of Justice. On the courthouse steps he stopped to address a waiting hoard of reporters, much to the horror of Pam Edstrom, his long time public relations spin meister, who had just noticed that Judge Thomas Penfield Jackson, the Federal Judge who ordered the breakup of Microsoft, was standing nearby and listing intently to every word of Bill's diatribe.

"The Department of Justice is completely wrong," railed the irate Gates. "They are a bunch of random twits led by an even larger random twit. These people are technological troglodytes who have no idea what they are talking about. This whole thing is a complete waste of time and money and I totally resent any implication that Microsoft has been hunting down and crushing our competitors using anything other than completely legal means."

"You shouldn't take this too seriously," said Edstrom sidling up to Judge Jackson and trying valiantly to regain control of the situation, "When he gets worked up like this Bill is sometimes really his own worst enemy."

"Not while I'm alive," replied the Judge.

(**Ed. Note:** the Microsoft breakup court order was vacated on appeal and Judge Jackson removed from the case; as of publication the issue remains unresolved.)

✦ ✦ ✦

Bill Gates was preparing to board a plane when he heard that the Pope was on the same flight. "This is cool," thought Bill. "I've always been curious about the Pope. Perhaps I'll be able to see him or even talk to him in person."

Imagine Bill's surprise when the Holy Father sat down in the seat next to him for the flight. Shortly after takeoff, the Pope began a crossword puzzle. "This is fantastic," thought Bill. "I'm really good at crosswords. If he gets stuck maybe he'll ask me to help."

Sure enough, almost immediately the Pope turned to Bill and said, "Excuse me my son, but do you know a five letter word referring to an unpleasant woman and that ends in the letters 'itch'?"

Only one word leapt to mind ... "Hmmm...," thought Bill, "I can't tell the Pope that. There must be another word." Bill wracked his brain for a while then it hit him. Triumphant, he turned to the Pope and said, "Your Holiness, I think the word you're looking for is 'witch'."

"Oooooh, of course!" replied the Pontiff. "Thank you my son. By the way, do you have an eraser?"

✦ ✦ ✦

## BILL'S LIMERICK

A software tycoon name of Gates
Found lawyers at Justice irate
A law suit ensued
And when it was through
Less rich, he now makes license plates

Traveling across Europe by train, Bill Gates finds himself sharing a first class cabin with Apple co-founder Steve Jobs, CNN reporter Paula Zahn and English actress/supermodel Elizabeth Hurley. The train goes into a long tunnel and suddenly the lights go out. After a few minutes the sound of a passionate kiss is heard, followed by a sharp slap. When the lights come back on no one says a thing but there is obviously a large, red welt on Bill's cheek.

Paula Zahn thinks, "Good for Elizabeth. I'd have slapped him myself. Hmmmmmm ..... I wonder if I should use this on my next American Morning show?"

Elizabeth Hurley thinks, "I can't believe he kissed her instead of me."

Bill Gates thinks, "Just my luck. Steve steals a kiss from one of the most beautiful women in the world and I get slapped on the snout."

Steve Jobs thinks, "What a killer deal! I kiss the back of my hand and get to slap Bill Gates across the mouth!!"

Bill Gates, on tour to promote his newly published autobiography, appears on the *Tonight Show*. After the usual introductory banter between Bill, Jay and Jay's other guest – a beautiful young starlet - Leno asks Bill, "You're the richest man in the world. What has your incredible success taught you about life?"

After thinking a moment, Bill responds, "I think I've learned that anyone can be successful if they are aggressive and persistent. Look at me. I've been successful in spite of having to overcome some serious limitations. For example, I was only born upper middle class. I need glasses. I only have average looks. But to compensate for these limitations, God gave me near perfection in brains, wit and charm."

"Oh, that's so wonderful," cooed the starlet, leaning toward Bill and wriggling seductively. "What else?"

"Well, let's see. I have an unerring sense of new technology and I can spot business trends well in advance of others," continued Bill as he glanced furtively at the attentive beauty next to him.

"Oh, I wish I understood all that technical stuff," she bubbled, hanging on his every word.

"I also have a unique insight into people's abilities and talents, I ..., I ..., I ..., blah ...blah ...blah ...," Bill rambled on and on, drawn out and encouraged by the beautiful young beauty's rapt attention.

Finally, after listening for a while, Jay turned to the audience, rolled his eyes and deadpanned, "Well ladies and gentlemen, this certainly proves it: If you stroke it, the thing that increases in size the most on a man is his ego."

Bill and Melinda were attending an air show at Boeing Field in Seattle when Bill, who had never been up in a stunt plane, became so fascinated by the aerobatic maneuvers being demonstrated that he decided to ask one of the stunt pilots how much a demo ride would cost.

"$150 for 20 minutes," replied the pilot of a vintage restored Stearman Kaydet N2S-5 open cockpit biplane.

Bill, interested but never one to take the first offer on any deal, said, "Hmmm .... that sounds pretty high."

Amused, the pilot thought for a second and then said, "OK, I'll make you a deal. If you and your wife fly for the full 20 minutes without screaming or uttering a sound, the ride's free. But if either of you makes any sound at all, you have to pay me the $150."

After a brief discussion Bill and Melinda agreed, squeezed into the front cockpit and off they went. Twisting, turning, rolls, loops - the pilot gave them a thrilling flight. After landing, the pilot said to Bill, "I want to congratulate you for not making a sound. I thought I had a sure thing. Most novices, can't take a ride like that without a few screams."

"Thank you," said Bill, "But I'll tell you, it was all I could do to keep from screaming when Melinda fell out."

## 10 Bill Gates impulse purchase ideas:

10. Spain

9. Space shuttle Atlantis

8. Smithsonian Institute

7. PGA Tour

6. Hearst Castle (decided to build, instead)

5. Yacht conversion for U.S.S. Nimitz

4. U.S. Department of Justice

3. Surplus Soviet SS19 10 MIRV nuclear tipped ICBM re-targeted at intersection of Middlefield Road and Ellis Street, Mountain View, California

   (Ed. Note: This location is in the middle of the AOL/Netscape corporate campus.)

2. Judge Thomas Penfield Jackson voodoo doll

1. Contact lenses

Bill Gates, venture capitalist John Doerr and PC industry author Robert X. Cringely are shipwrecked and cast adrift in shark infested waters. Their raft has drifted tantalizingly close to shore but the tide makes it impossible for them to paddle to the beach. There is no choice: they are going to have to swim for it or be swept out to sea.

Cringely decides to go first. Stripping down to his shorts, he gathers his strength waits until the sharks are on the far side of the boat and jumps into the water. The sharks turn to pursue but, having caught them by surprise, Cringely puts on a surprising burst of speed and scrambles ashore just in time.

Doerr decides to go next. There is no fooling the sharks again, however, and as he jumps into the water there is a mad swirling as the sharks converge. Expecting to see him torn to shreds, Gates is amazed to see Doerr rise to the surface seated on one of the largest sharks who safely conveys him to shore.

Finally, it's Bill's turn. As he gets up in the boat, from the shore Cringely and Doerr are amazed to see the sharks line up together to form a bridge. Walking on sharks pressed fin to fin from boat to beach, Gates strolls ashore without so much as getting his feet wet.

Safe on shore at last, they compare stories.

"I'm a strong swimmer," said Cringely, "So I knew I had a good chance of making it. But why did the sharks help the two of you?"

Doerr looked at them both with a smile and answered, "Professional courtesy."

Gates in turn flashed a toothy grin and replied, "Family ties."

The mean distance from the earth to the moon is approximately 238,906 miles. As of January, 2002, Bill Gates' Microsoft stock was worth approximately $41 billion (it typically goes up or down a billion or two each day!). In single dollar bills laid end to end that is enough to stretch from the earth to the moon 16.59 times. And that's no joke!!

✦ ✦ ✦

Bill Gates, tiring of being the butt of so many jokes, hires private investigators to locate the source. After an exhaustive search, they locate the culprit and Gates decides to confront him in person. "Are you responsible for that joke about me ending up in Hell after selecting it from the demo?" Gates demanded.

"Yup."

"How about the stupid one where the boy saves me from drowning and is afraid his uncle Steve Case will kill him for saving me??"

"Mine, too."

"What about that really lame one about my getting slapped on the face by Steve Jobs during a train ride???"

"Right, again."

**"HOW DARE YOU DO THIS YOU RANDOM, PRESUMPTUOUS TWIT??"** yells Bill, going ballistic. **"I'M BILL GATES. I'M THE RICHEST MAN IN THE WORLD. BEFORE I'M THROUGH MICROSOFT WILL BE THE BIGGEST, THE MOST SUCCESSFUL, THE MOST VALUABLE, THE MOST INFLUENTIAL COMPANY THE WORLD HAS EVER SEEN. . ."**

"Now wait a minute," said the joker, interrupting Bill's tirade. "That one isn't mine...."

✦ ✦ ✦

# 7.0    Windows Glossary - 200+ Special Terms Defined

**Winappropriate** - Has a chance of working with Windows

**Wincantation** - Prayer to the Gods that Windows loads and runs

**Wincapable** - PC with adequate resources to run Windows

**Wincapacitate** - What happens when you try to run too many applications at once.

**Wincense** - What you burn when doing the Wincantation

**Wincinerate** - What a lot of users would like to do to their copies of Windows

**Wincite** - Any place where Windows has been installed

**Wincivility** - Normal Microsoft behavior toward other developers

**Wincognito** - Microsoft Windows developers who secretly use a Macintosh

**Wincoherent** - Early Microsoft Windows strategy

**Wincome** - Revenue Microsoft gets from the sale of Windows

**Wincommunicable** - Windows virus

**Wincommunicato** - How you are when dial up networking fails

**Wincompatible** - Claims to work with Windows

**Wincompetent** - The Windows development team

**Wincomplete** - The permanent state of Windows

**Wincompliant** - Meets appropriate Windows specifications

**Wincomprehensible** - Most Windows documentation

**Wincomputable** - Something simple enough for Windows to get done in a reasonable amount of time

# The↗ Unauthorized Microsoft Joke Book - 2<sup>nd</sup> Edition

**Winconceivable** - The notion that anyone actually bought BOB.

**Winconsequential** - Microsoft's view of non-Windows software

**Winconsistent** - Follows the Windows API rules faithfully

**Winconsolable** - Most Macintosh users

**Wincontestable** - Windows influence on the entire PC industry

**Wincontinent** - The landfill where unsold copies of BOB were dumped

**Winconvenient** - An oxymoron

**Wincorporation** - Microsoft

**Wincorrigible** - What the Department of Justice thinks of Microsoft business practices

**Wincorruptible** - What you hope your Windows registry is

**Wincrease** - What the size of Windows does, release after release

**Wincredible** - That any of it works at all

**Wincriminate** - What the Department of Justice hopes its box cars of evidence will do to Microsoft

**Wincubate** - Place Windows developers in special office space

**Wincubus** - Special demon assigned to make life hell for Windows users

**Wincur** - Dog that really hates Windows users

**Wincurable** - There is no uninstall program for Windows

**Wincursion** - When Windows starts taking over your other hard disk partitions

**Windebted** - What you will be by the time you buy everything you need to run Windows XP effectively.

**Windecent** - Microsoft's profits on Windows

**Windecipherable** - Most Windows registry entries

**Windecision** - To upgrade or not to upgrade, that is the question.

**Windecorous** - Member of a group that sings about Windows

**Windefatigable** - Microsoft quest to promote Windows

**Windefinite** - Release date of most new Microsoft products

**Windemnification** - What Microsoft needs to protect itself

**Windent** - Result of throwing Office Pro retail package at bus

**Windependent** - How Microsoft wants all PC owners

**Windescribable** - Normal Windows product documentation

**Windestructible** - Any data when Windows is running

**Windict** - U.S. Department of Justice objective for Microsoft

**Windignant** - How Bill Gates feels about U.S. Department of Justice objective for Microsoft

**Windiscernible** - Advantages of Windows XP over Windows ME

**Windiscrete** - Internet Explorer inadvertently broadcasts your collection of XXX rated bookmarks mail onto the Internet

**Windiscriminant** - The slaughter of previously installed software when a new Microsoft application is installed

**Windispose** - What many users would do if they could

**Windividual** - Each and every owner of Windows

**Windoctrinate** - Mission of the Microsoft PR machine

**Windomitable** - Microsoft's will to win

**Winduce** - In solitaire, played on the Wintrey

**Windustrial** - Original plan for Windows NT

**Winebriated** - Drunken state of Macintosh users after being told their shop is changing to Windows

**Wineffective** - Something Windows actually does well

**Winelegant** - A contradiction in terms

**Winept** - Most developers when first starting to write for Windows

**Winequality** - Windows is an equal opportunity system trasher

**Winescapable** - Windows in the workplace

**Winestimable** - Media storage space used since Windows introduced

**Winevitable** - Microsoft's takeover of the world economy

**Winexcusable** - There's an excuse for this thing?

**Winexhaustible** - Supply of programmers who want to work at Microsoft

**Winexorable** - Bill Gates' drive to make Windows succeed

**Winexpensive** - The total cost after you add up upgrade after upgrade after upgrade....

**Winexperience** - Usually negative at first, may improve some with time

**Winexplicable** - The way lots and lots of things happen in Windows

**Winextinguishable** - Hope among the Linux community

**Winextricable** - The linkage of Microsoft and Intel's fates

**Winfallible** - Any Papal pronouncements regarding Windows

**Winfamous** - Microsoft itself

**Winfamy** - What August 24, 1995, will live on in (**Ed. note**: that was the introduction date of Windows 95)

**Winfantile** - Microsoft behavior when thwarted

**Winfantry** - Microsoft programming corps

**Winfatuation** - Unrealistic initial enchantment with Windows

**Winfection** - A virus invasion of Windows (not to be confused with Windows itself)

**Winferior** - Microsoft's view of other software companies

**Winfernal** - Other software company's view of Microsoft

**Winferno** - What's you'd have if you burned all unsold copies of BOB

**Winfest** - Microsoft sponsored Windows event

**Winfidel** - Macintosh user

**Winfinite** - Microsoft's ambitions for Windows

**Winfirm** - see Wincorporation

**Winflammable** - If all else fails, the disks and manuals DO burn

**Winflate** - Microsoft's approach to promoting Window's features

**Winflexible** - Another oxymoron

**Winflict** - To install Windows without the victims permission

**Winfluence** - What Bill Gates buys with political contributions

**Winfluenza** - Special form of Windows computer virus

**Winformant** - Spy placed inside a software developing competitor

**Winfrastructure** - Microsoft Windows development group

**Winfringe** - The outlying limits of Windows development

**Winfuriate** - Tell Bill Gates that Windows looks "just like a Mac"

**Winfusion** - Melding of inferior design with mediocre technology

**Wingenuity** - What it takes to work around a lot of Windows features

**Wingratitude** - What Microsoft treated IBM with

**Wingrown** - and grown and grown....

**Winhabit** - Can't turn off that Windows PC

**Winhospitable** - Yet another oxymoron

**Winhumane** - Making an animal use Windows

**Winitial** - In the beginning there was the Xerox Star...

**Winitiate** - Boot up Windows

**Winitiative** - Key trait of Microsoft personnel

**Winjunction** - What the justice department wishes it could get

**Winjure** - What the justice department says Microsoft has done

**Winjustice** - What the justice department is unlikely to get

**Winland** - Redmond/Bellevue, Washington

**Winlay** - <censored>

**Winner** - In the end, likely Microsoft outcome in the anti-trust case

**Winnocent** - Something considerably different from 'Not Guilty'

**Winnovate** - Yet another oxymoron

**Winnuendo** - Use FUD (Fear, Uncertainty, Doubt) against competitors

**Winnumerable** - Lots and lots of Windows applications out there

**Winoculate** - Install Windows anti-virus protection

**Winoffensive** - Microsoft campaign to make Windows the world standard

**Winoperable** - How Windows renders some computer systems

**Winorganic** - Windows 2007

**Winput** - What Microsoft gets a lot of from frustrated users

**Winquest** - see Winoffensive

**Winquire** - Call Windows technical support for help

**Winquisition** - Microsoft's view of the justice department investigation

**Winroad** - Washington State Highways 202 and 908

**Winsane** - What trying to fix Windows problems can drive you

**Winsatiable** - Bill Gates quest for power

**Winscribe** - Windows staff technical writer

**Winsect** - Typical Windows bug

**Winsecticide** - Typical Windows debugger

**Winsecure** - Yet another oxymoron

**Winsenstate** - User after non-stop 26 hour Windows session

**Winsensitive** - How Microsoft reacts to criticism of Windows

**Winset** - Microsoft Office in all its wincarnations

**Winshore** - The Mercer Island beach on Lake Washington

**Winside** - Opposite of Woutside

**Winsidious** - The takeover of the earth by Microsoft

**Winsight** - A higher level view of Windows in the grand scheme of things

**Winsignia** - The Windows splash page

**Winsignificant** - How Microsoft sees all other software developers

**Winsincere** - If you can fake this, you can fake anything

**Winsinuate** - Imply Windows can do something

**Winsipid** - Microsoft content standard

**Winsist** - Demand Windows on a new system

**Winsofar** - So far, so good?

**Winsolent** - This book

**Winsomnia** - Comes from using Windows too long at a session

**Winspect** - Original Windows design document

**Winstability** - Yet another oxymoron

**Winstall** - When Windows crashes for no apparent reason

**Winstantaneous** - Something happens real fast (for Windows)

**Winstate** - Washington (the one north of Oregon, not D.C.)

**Winstinct** - It stinked then and it stinks now

**Winstitute** - Microsoft University

**Winstruct** - To teach the basics of Windows to new users

**Winstrument** - Supports the Windows MIDI interface

**Winsubordinate** - Status of all other PC software developers

**Winsubstantial** - Microsoft view of all other PC software developers

**Winsufferable** - Other PC developers view of Microsoft

**Winsufficient** - A computer capable of running Windows

**Winsult** - Tell a Mac user that it's "Just like Windows"

**Winsupportable** - Might work with Windows, might not.

**Winsurmountable** - Windows position in software market

**Winsurrection** - What it will finally take to overthrow Windows in the software market

**Winsusceptible** - A dissatisfied Macintosh user

**Wintact** - Normally lacking in Microsoft relations with developers

**Wintake** - And keeps on taking

**Wintangible** - The advantages of Windows XP over Windows ME

**Wintegral** - A piece of code necessary for Windows to run

**Wintegration** - Building more and more apps into Windows

**Wintegrity** - Not a trait for which Microsoft is known

**Wintelligent** - Microsoft and Intel working together

**Wintend** - To maintain Windows

**Wintense** - The emotions Windows generates in both users and detractors

**Wintent** - Where Microsoft holds outdoor product launches

**Wintercede** - What Microsoft competitors want the Department of Justice to do

**Winterest** - New user curiosity about Windows

**Winterface** - Get a mouse. Learn to use it.

**Winterim** - All the Windows releases between the 'big' numbers

**Wintern** - Windows doctor in training

**Winternational** - The spread of Windows around the world

**Winterstellar** - The spread of Window throughout the galaxy
**Winterval** - Time between new releases of Windows

**Wintervene** - What the Department of Justice is trying to do

**Winterview** - Bill Gates on a talk show

**Wintolerable** - Barely

## TOTALLY
# The↗ Unauthorized Microsoft Joke Book - 2nd Edition

**Wintroduction** - Windows release launch festivities

**Wintuitive** - A Macintosh

**Winundate** - What a Microsoft Windows launch does to the media

**Winvasion** - The spread of Windows in the home and workplace

**Winvent** - Where you let the steam out of all the Windows claims

**Winverse** - Poem to or about Windows

**Winvestigation** - U.S. Justice Department's ongoing activity

**Winvitation** - Opportunity to attend a Microsoft Windows event

**Winvocation** - see Wincantation

**Winvoice** - Talking Windows - Oh, Goody!

**Winvulnerable** - How Microsoft perceives itself

**Winward** - Hospital ward for geeks OD'd on Windows

## 8.   BONUS CHAPTER - 101 Classic Light Bulb Jokes

They're not all about Microsoft but here are some of the "best and brightest" light bulb jokes we've collected over the years....Enjoy.

Q.   How many tenured professors does it take to change a light bulb?
A.   None. That's what student research assistants are for.

✦ ✦ ✦

Q.   How many actors does it take to change a light bulb?
A.   One, but 146 showed up for the audition.

✦ ✦ ✦

Q.   How many real estate appraisers does it take to change a light bulb?
A.   How many do you need it to be?

✦ ✦ ✦

Q.   How many Florida voters does it take to change a light bulb?
A.   Nobody knows for sure - they're still counting.

✦ ✦ ✦

Q.   How many politically correct workers does it take to change a light bulb?
A.   None. There is no such thing as a burned out bulb – they are just "illumination challenged"

✦ ✦ ✦

Q.   How many light beer drinkers does it take to change a light bulb?
A.   About one third less than for a regular bulb.

✦ ✦ ✦

Q.   How many astronomers does it take to change a light bulb?
A.   None. Astronomers prefer the dark.

✦ ✦ ✦

Q.   How many computer programmers does it take to change a light bulb?
A.   Two - one always leaves in the middle of a project.

✦ ✦ ✦

**Q.** How many ego maniacs does it take to change a light bulb?
**A.** One. They just hold onto the bulb and wait for the world to revolve around them.

✦ ✦ ✦

**Q.** How many archaeologists does it take to change a light bulb?
**A.** Three. One to change the bulb and two to stand around arguing about the age of the old bulb.

✦ ✦ ✦

**Q.** How many fishermen does it take to change a light bulb?
**A.** Only one, but you should've seen the bulb that got away! It must have been this big!

✦ ✦ ✦

**Q.** How many modern art critics does it take to change a light bulb?
**A.** Two. One to do it and one to say "My five-year old could do better than that."

✦ ✦ ✦

**Q.** How many atheists does it take to change a light bulb?
**A.** None. Atheists never see the light.

✦ ✦ ✦

**Q.** How many valley girls does it take to change a light bulb?
**A.** What? And wreck my nails?

✦ ✦ ✦

**Q.** How many building contractors does it take to change a light bulb?
**A.** Forty-seven. One to hold the bulb, one to get the permits, 45 to turn the house around.

✦ ✦ ✦

**Q.** How many alcoholics anonymous members does it take to change a light bulb?
**A.** One, but it takes twelve steps.

✦ ✦ ✦

**Q.** How many economists does it take to change a light bulb?
**A.** None. If the light bulb really needed changing, market forces would have already caused it to change.

✦ ✦ ✦

**Q.** How many Mafia hitmen does it take to change a light bulb?
**A.** Three. One to change the bulb, one to stand guard and one to shoot any witnesses.

✦ ✦ ✦

**Q.** How many bureaucrats does it take to change a light bulb?
**A.** Thirty-five. Five to form a committee to determine the bulb is really needs to be changed, three to prepare the bid proposal for vendors to submit to supply the replacement bulb, five to verify all potential bulb vendors comply with OSHA, ERISA, ADA and all other applicable regulations, five to perform the environmental impact study, one to award the contract to supply the replacement bulb to the winning vendor, one to change the bulb, five to write the final report to Congress and ten to complete the paperwork reduction act paperwork.

✦ ✦ ✦

**Q.** How many Californians does it take to change a light bulb?
**A.** Six. One to change the bulb, one for support and four to share the experience.

✦ ✦ ✦

**Q.** How many Oregonians does it take to change a light bulb?
**A.** Three. One to change the bulb, one to hold the umbrella and one to fight off the Californians trying to share the experience.

✦ ✦ ✦

**Q.** How many women with PMS does it take to change a light bulb?
**A.** One. Only ONE!! And do you know WHY it takes only ONE? Because NO ONE else in this house knows HOW to change a light bulb. They don't even notice the bulb is BURNED OUT. They sit in the dark for days before they notice. And once they notice they don't know WHERE to find the light bulbs DESPITE the fact that they've been on the SAME SHELF for the past SIX YEARS. But if BY SOME MIRACLE they did actually find them, two days LATER the chair they

stood on to change the stupid bulb would STILL BE IN THE SAME SPOT! AND ON THE **FLOOR** UNDERNEATH IT WOULD BE THE **BULB WRAPPER!!** WHY? BECAUSE NO ONE IN THIS HOUSE **EVER** PUTS **ANYTHING** IN THE TRASH OR **CARRIES OUT THE GARBAGE!! IT'S A MIRACLE WE ALL HAVEN'T BEEN SUFFOCATED BY THE PILES OF GARBAGE ALL OVER THIS HOUSE!! IT WOULD TAKE WEEKS JUST TO CLEAN ......** I'm sorry ...... what did you just ask me? .........

✦ ✦ ✦

**Q.** How many Chinese does it take to change a light bulb?
**A.** Several hundred. Confucius says many hands make light work.

✦ ✦ ✦

**Q.** How many researchers does it take to change a light bulb?
**A.** Five. One to write a grant proposal, one to do the mathematical model, one to type a research paper, one to submit the paper for publication and one to hire a student to do the work.

✦ ✦ ✦

**Q.** How many chiropractors does it take to change a light bulb?
**A.** One, but it takes ten visits to make sure it stays changed.

✦ ✦ ✦

**Q.** How many antique dealers does it take to change a light bulb?
**A.** Two. One to remove the bulb and one to find a candle that fits the socket.

✦ ✦ ✦

**Q.** How many consultants does it take to change a light bulb?
**A.** I'll have an estimate for you a week from Monday.

✦ ✦ ✦

**Q.** How many dentists does it take to change a light bulb?
**A.** Three. One to extract the dead light bulb, one to offer the empty socket some vile mouthwash and one to fit the new bulb.

✦ ✦ ✦

**Q.** How many doctors does it take to change a light bulb?
**A.** Two. One to change the bulb and one to sign the death certificate for the old bulb.

◆ ◆ ◆

**Q.** How many serious drinkers does it take to change a light bulb?
**A.** Ten. One to hold the bulb and nine to drink until the room spins.

◆ ◆ ◆

**Q.** How many Bob Dylan fans does it take to change a light bulb?
**A.** The answer, my friend, is blowin' in the wind.

◆ ◆ ◆

**Q.** How many dyslexics does it take to change a light bulb?
**A.** enO.

◆ ◆ ◆

**Q.** How many efficiency experts does it take to change a light bulb?
**A.** None. Efficiency experts only replace dim bulbs.

◆ ◆ ◆

**Q.** How many scientists does it take to change a light bulb near the speed of light?
**A.** It depends on the speed of the changer and the mass of the bulb. Or vice versa. Then again, it might be easier to leave the bulb alone and change the room. It's all relative.

◆ ◆ ◆

**Q.** How many Elvis fans does it take to change a light bulb?
**A.** None. No bulb will ever burn as brightly as the old one.

◆ ◆ ◆

**Q.** How many aerospace engineers does it take to change a light bulb?
**A.** None. It's not rocket science, you know.

◆ ◆ ◆

**Q.** How many ergonomists does it take to change a light bulb?
**A.** Five. One to decide which way the bulb ought to turn, one to

calculate the force required to turn it, one to design a tool to turn the bulb, one to change the bulb and one to design warning labels for the socket.

✦ ✦ ✦

**Q.** How many militant feminists does it take to change a light bulb?
**A.** Two. One to change the bulb and one to tell any man in sight to, "GET LOST" just in case they to volunteer to help.

✦ ✦ ✦

**Q.** How many firefighters does it take to change a light bulb?
**A.** Four. Three to cut a hole in the roof and one to climb down and change the bulb.

✦ ✦ ✦

**Q.** How many pipe fitters does it take to change a light bulb?
**A.** None. That's an electrician's job.

✦ ✦ ✦

**Q.** How many gay men does it take to change a light bulb?
**A.** Three. One to screw in an art deco bulb and two to shriek "Fabulous!"

✦ ✦ ✦

**Q.** How many gay rights activists does it take to change a light bulb?
**A.** None. No bulb should have to change for society to accept it.

✦ ✦ ✦

**Q.** How many Gods does it take to change a light bulb?
**A.** Two. One to hold the bulb and the other to rotate the planet.

✦ ✦ ✦

**Q.** How many gorillas does it take to change a light bulb?
**A.** One (but it takes a lot of light bulbs!).

✦ ✦ ✦

**Q.** How many hippies does it take to change a light bulb?
**A.** Oh, WOW, is it, like, dark, man?

✦ ✦ ✦

**Q.**    How many Hell's Angels does it take to change a light bulb?
**A.**    Eighteen or more. One to change the bulb and the others to kick the shit out of the switch.

✦ ✦ ✦

**Q.**    How many movie directors does it take to change a light bulb?
**A.**    Just one, but he needs at least 12 takes.

✦ ✦ ✦

**Q.**    How many tree huggers does it take to change a light bulb?
**A.**    None. If the light bulb is out, that's the way Nature intended it!

✦ ✦ ✦

**Q.**    How many historians does it take to change a light bulb?
**A.**    Ten. One to do change the bulb and nine to document it for posterity.

✦ ✦ ✦

**Q.**    How many NASA space shuttle technicians does it take to change a light bulb?
**A.**    Twenty. They plan it for weeks and when they finally get around to it the weather is bad so they have to postpone the change for another week. Also, the light bulbs cost $2.6 million dollars each.

✦ ✦ ✦

**Q.**    How many NASA scientists does it take to change a light bulb?
**A.**    Forget light bulbs, that technology is obsolete. For a mere $100 billion or so, we plan to put up a chain of geosynchronous plasma satellites that will illuminate the whole planet.

✦ ✦ ✦

**Q.**    How many evolutionists does it take to change a light bulb?
**A.**    Only one, but it takes several million years.

✦ ✦ ✦

**Q.**    How many creationists does it take to change a light bulb?
**A.**    Only one, but it requires divine intervention.

✦ ✦ ✦

**Q.** How many holocaust revisionists does it take to change a light bulb?
**A.** None. They just deny the bulb was ever lit in the first place.

✦ ✦ ✦

**Q.** How many homophobes does it take to change a light bulb?
**A.** None. They'd really prefer that the bulbs stayed in the closet.

✦ ✦ ✦

**Q.** How many members of an Honor Guard does it take to change a light bulb?
**A.** Twenty-two. One to change the bulb, 21 to shoot it.

✦ ✦ ✦

**Q.** How many youth gang members does it take to change a light bulb?
**A.** Four. One to rob the liquor store to get money for the bulb, one to drive the getaway car, one to change the bulb, and one to hold his crack pipe while he does it.

✦ ✦ ✦

**Q.** How many jugglers does it take to change a light bulb?
**A.** One, but it takes at least three light bulbs.

✦ ✦ ✦

**Q.** How many lawyers does it take to change a light bulb?
**A.** Three. One to change the bulb while two to keep interrupting by shouting "Objection".

✦ ✦ ✦

**Q.** How many revolutionaries does it take to change a light bulb?
**A.** Revolutionaries don't change light bulbs, they change the entire system.

✦ ✦ ✦

**Q.** How many AOL users does it take to change a light bulb?
**A.** Three. One to change the bulb, one to send instant message announcements to everybody and one to monitor the bulb newsgroup.

✦ ✦ ✦

# TOTALLY
## The Unauthorized Microsoft Joke Book - 2<sup>nd</sup> Edition

**Q.** How many lesbians does it take to change a light bulb?
**A.** Five. One to change it and the other four to sit around and discuss how it's so much more gratifying than a man.

✦ ✦ ✦

**Q.** How many Libertarians does it take to change a light bulb?
**A.** None, because somebody might come into the room who likes to sit in the dark.

✦ ✦ ✦

**Q.** How many Microsoft executives does it take to change a light bulb?
**A.** Eight. One to change the bulb and seven to make sure that Microsoft gets $2 for every light bulb changed anywhere in the world.

✦ ✦ ✦

**Q.** How many Microsoft technical support staff members does it take to change a light bulb?
**A.** Four. One to ask, "What is the registration number of the light bulb?", one to ask, "Have you tried rebooting it?", another to ask, "Have you tried reinstalling it?" and the last one to say, "It must be your hardware because the light bulb in our office works fine ..."

✦ ✦ ✦

**Q.** How many procrastinators does it take to change a light bulb?
**A.** One, but they always wait for the light to get better.

✦ ✦ ✦

**Q.** How many Microsoft vice presidents does it take to change a light bulb?
**A.** None. Microsoft will simply redefine darkness as the industry standard.

✦ ✦ ✦

**Q.** How many missionaries does it take to change a light bulb?
**A.** One hundred and one. One to change the bulb and 100 to convince everyone else to change light bulbs, too.

✦ ✦ ✦

**Q.** How many mystery writers does it take to change a light bulb?
**A.** Two. One to screw it almost all the way in and the other to give it a surprising twist at the end.

✦ ✦ ✦

**Q.** How many nuclear engineers does it take to change a light bulb?
**A.** Five. One to change the bulb and six to figure out what to do with the old bulb for the next 10,000 years.

✦ ✦ ✦

**Q.** How many Chernobyl survivors does it take to change a light bulb?
**A.** None. People who glow in the dark don't need light bulbs.

✦ ✦ ✦

**Q.** How many optimists does it take to change a light bulb?
**A.** None. They all believe the power will come back on soon.

✦ ✦ ✦

**Q.** How many pessimists does it take to change a light bulb?
**A.** None. They would rather sit in the dark.

✦ ✦ ✦

**Q.** How many IBM strategists does it take to change a light bulb?
**A.** Eleven. One to change the bulb and ten to write document number LB671134-0001, "Single User Incandescent Illumination Peripheral Device, Maintenance Instructions".

✦ ✦ ✦

**Q.** How many poets does it take to change a light bulb?
**A.** Three. One to curse the darkness, one to light a candle and one to change the bulb and write iambic pentameter about how the experience changed their perspective on life.

✦ ✦ ✦

**Q.** How many police officers does it take to change a light bulb?
**A.** None. The bulb turned itself in.

✦ ✦ ✦

**Q.**   How many political activists does it take to change a light bulb?
**A.**   Two. One to do change the bulb and one to pass out pamphlets.

✦ ✦ ✦

**Q.**   How many Oracle engineers does it take to change a light bulb?
**A.**   Three. One to write a bulb removal program, one to write a bulb installation program and one socket administrator to control socket access and make sure nobody else tries to change the bulb at the same time.

✦ ✦ ✦

**Q.**   How many politicians does it take to change a light bulb?
**A.**   Three. One to change the bulb and two to promise that everything possible is being done to solve the problem.

✦ ✦ ✦

**Q.**   How many psychiatrists does it take to change a light bulb?
**A.**   One, but the light bulb must genuinely want to change.

✦ ✦ ✦

**Q.**   How many psychoanalysts does it take to change a light bulb?
**A.**   Two. One to change the bulb and one to complain how psychoanalysts don't get the respect they deserve like psychiatrists.

✦ ✦ ✦

**Q.**   How many real men does it take to change a light bulb?
**A.**   None. Real men aren't afraid of the dark.

✦ ✦ ✦

**Q.**   How many quantum physicists does it take to change a light bulb?
**A.**   None. If they know where the bulb is they can't find the socket.

✦ ✦ ✦

**A.**   One.
**Q.**   How many psychics does it take to change a light bulb?

✦ ✦ ✦

**Q.** How many Democrats does it take to change a light bulb?
**A.** Two. One to change the bulb and Tom Daschel to denounce the change and point out that more light unfairly favors the very richest 10% of all Americans.

✦ ✦ ✦

**Q.** How many Republicans does it take to change a light bulb?
**A.** Two. One to change the bulb and Tom DeLay to denounce the change and point out that widely scattered light is just another left wing entitlement program.

✦ ✦ ✦

**Q.** How many spies does it take to change a light bulb?
**A.** Two. One to change the bulb and the other to check for bugs.

✦ ✦ ✦

**Q.** How many square dancers does it take to change a light bulb?
**A.** Four, but you have to walk them through it a few times.

✦ ✦ ✦

**Q.** How many medical school students does it take to change a light bulb?
**A.** Five. One to change the bulb while fighting off the four trying to pull the ladder out from under him.

✦ ✦ ✦

**Q.** How many terrorists does it take to change a light bulb?
**A.** Two. One to stage a suicide attack on the bulb and another to claim responsibility in a phone call to the news media.

✦ ✦ ✦

**Q.** How many ER doctors does it take to change a light bulb?
**A.** One, but the bulb will have to spend four hours in the waiting room.

✦ ✦ ✦

**Q.** How many meter maids does it take to change a light bulb?
**A.** Two. One to change the bulb and one to give the old bulb a ticket for staying on too long.

✦ ✦ ✦

**Q.**     How many Windows users does it take to change a light bulb?
**A.**     Two. One to change the bulb and one to swear that the bulb is as easy to change as it is on a Macintosh.

✦ ✦ ✦

**Q.**     How many Macintosh users does it take to change a light bulb?
**A.**     Two. One to change the bulb and one to swear that it would take at least twice as long for a Windows user.

✦ ✦ ✦

**Q.**     How many Zen masters does it take to change a light bulb?
**A.**     Two. One to change the bulb, and one not to change it

✦ ✦ ✦

**Q.**     How many WWF wrestlers does it take to change a light bulb?
**A.**     Three. One to yank out the old bulb, throw it on the floor, jump on it and then act surprised when it rolls out of the way at the last minute, one to twist the new bulb into the socket so far that it almost breaks and a referee to be completely ignored by the two wrestlers.

✦ ✦ ✦

**Q.**     How many union electricians does it take to change a light bulb?
**A.**     Ten. One to climb the ladder and remove the old bulb. One to hold him on the stepladder. Four to steady the stepladder. One to dispose of the old bulb. One to unpack a new bulb and give it to the installer. One to turn on the switch to test the bulb. One shop steward to supervise and make sure all breaks are taken on time.

✦ ✦ ✦

**Q.**     How many Windows programmers does it take to change a light bulb?
**A.**     None - it is clearly a hardware problem.

✦ ✦ ✦

**Q.**     How many R&D engineers does it take to change a light bulb?
**A.**     Only one, but if you just wait another month we'll be out with a much better bulb.

✦ ✦ ✦

**Q.** How many ENRON executives does it take to change a light bulb?
**A.** Who knows?  We thought the Anderson auditors could tell us!!

◆ ◆ ◆

**Q.** How many members of your Zodiac sign does it take to change a light bulb?

**A.** AQUARIUS: Lots - all competing to bring illumination to the world.

**A.** PISCES: There's a light bulb out?

**A.** ARIES: One. Just one. You want to make something out of it?

**A.** TAURUS: One, but only if they can celebrate afterward with a huge feast and some great sex.

**A.** GEMINI: Two, but the light bulb never gets changed - they just keep arguing about who is supposed to change it and how it's supposed to be done!

**A.** CANCER: One, but it takes a therapist three years to help them through their grief process.

**A.** LEO: Leos don't change light bulbs, although sometime they get a Virgo to do it for them.

**A.** VIRGO: Approximately 1.0000 with an error of 0.01% but normally Virgos don't have time to change their own light bulbs because they're too busy changing them for everybody else.

**A.** LIBRA: Hmmm...Let's see. Two. Or maybe one. No, on second thought, two. One. No, it's two. Is that OK with you?

**A.** SCORPIO: That information is strictly secret and shared only with the enlightened members of the Ancient Hierarchical Order.

**A.** SAGITTARIUS: A lot. Each Sagittarian only stays in the room long enough to give the bulb a quarter turn.

**A.** CAPRICORN: Capricorns don't waste time with childish jokes.

## 9. Dramatis Personae

Names, titles and starting page number of items featuring the principal characters in this book:

| | | |
|---|---|---|
| **Kildall, Gary** (1942-1994) | Founder, Digital Research, Developer of CP/M (an early DOS). A good friend, much missed. | 69 |
| **Leno, Jay** | Host, *Tonight Show*. Comedian. | 80 |
| **Limbaugh, Rush** | Famous political commentator and radio/TV personality | 31 |
| **Lopez, Jennifer** | Famous musician and actress | 31 |
| **Maher, Bill** | Talk show host and comedian | 31 |
| **Markoff, John** | Technology Reporter, *New York Times* | 40 |
| **McNealy, Scott** | Chairman, President and CEO, Sun Microsystems | 77 |
| **Myhrvold, Nathan** | Co-President, Intellectual Ventures | 41 |
| **Nader, Ralph** | Consumer Advocate | 39 |
| **Noorda, Ray** | Former President and CEO, Novell Corporation | 69 |
| **Raikes, Jeff** | Group Vice President, Microsoft Corporation | 11 |
| **Stern, Howard** | Famous radio personality | 31 |
| **Torquemada, Tomas** | Grand Inquisitor, Spanish Inquisition c. 1490 | 26 |
| **Torvalds, Linus** | Inventor, Linux | 47 |
| **Wallace, Mike** | Famous investigative TV Reporter, *60 Minutes* | 73 |
| **Zahn, Paula** | CNN reporter/news anchor | 79 |

## About the Editor

**Tim Barry** has been in and around the personal computer industry since 1974 when dinosaurs and 8080's ruled the earth. Starting out as a semiconductor engineer in Silicon Valley, his career has included a variety of positions in hardware/software product development, consulting and general management. Over the years he has had the opportunity to meet and work with a number of the individuals making character appearances in *The Totally Unauthorized Microsoft Joke Book.*

The holder of six patents; the author of three books plus numerous articles on the personal computer industry, the editor of over 50 computer books and a former *Infoworld* columnist, Mr. Barry was most recently President of UCI Web Group, Inc., an internationally recognized web development firm. He moved from Silicon Valley to southwest Washington in 1997 where he now consults, writes, serves on boards of directors and bores his friends with tales of the halcyon years of the personal computer industry. He founded Intelligent Technologies, Inc. in 1998 to develop a variety of products and market them via the Internet.